Blue
Pebbles
& Other
GIFTS
of
SPIRIT

Dreams, Intuition
and Synchronicity

Frances McMaster

ISBN: 1-4392-1622-3
ISBN-13: 9781439216224

to Carol — my friend and kindred spirit. I hope you enjoy reading this.

Frances McMaster

Dedication

This book is meant to be a hug for Jeremy, who has discovered the courage to embrace life rather than trying to escape it, and who found my words inspiring. May he know that he, in turn, helped inspire me to write it.

Acknowledgments

With enormous gratitude I thank Lynn Holubec the talented photographer who captured the beauty of my box of blue pebbles for the cover art. I am indebted to Amanda Mora Jones for her computer assistance. I want to thank the many people who contributed to the contents of this book, even if they may not realize that they did so. It has taken an extraordinary effort to pull the book together because of the length of time it covers, the many people I've known, and the multitudinous experiences that I have encountered on my life journey. My son Doc's urgings have possibly been the most insistent, but my daughter Sharon speaks the same language, has a deep understanding of my inner life, and has offered unyielding support. My grandchildren are enthusiastic about having a grandmother who has kept going for all these ages, which pleases and encourages me.

I must give credit to members of Author's Unlimited, the writer's group I attended for years in Houston for helping me hone my writing skills. My undying gratitude goes to Guida Jackson, author and publisher, who selected my mystery, "Death Plays the Lead", as the first book published by Panther Creek Press.

Particular thanks go to each of the people who were involved in my stories and especially to my friend Anna Renken Lafrenz of Fort Clark Springs who lived out some of these incidences with me and to my other friends at the Fort.

Two women who are members of the clergy were involved in separate incidences of unusual coincidences. Episcopal Bishop Dena Harrison touched my life many years ago and again recently in a very meaningful way. Methodist minister, Pastor Jean Reardon, played a major role in one of the recent and amazing synchronistic events recounted in the book.

Anna Carter of San Diego, California has become a significant person in my life as well as in the members of my family for which we are all grateful. Thanks go to those more directly involved in the writing process. Dr. Carrie Watson who as Director of Lay Ministries at St. Stephen's Episcopal Church introduced me to people she knew that I would like when I first came to Wimberley and encouraged me to speak my truth. I am indebted to my good friend Mary Anne McGee who is a great listener and patiently put up with my day-to-day progress reports on the book. I thank the members of the Jung Study Group who unwittingly listened to a lot of the book's contents in the course of our discussions and put up with my ramblings. My special gratitude goes to Jo Bourke, Editor of the St. Stephen's Devotionals, who served as my book editor as well as to friends Margaret Kimble and Marilyn Hazlet who read through the book prior to publication to tell me if it made sense.

St. Stephen's Father Patrick Gahan has earned my deep gratitude for inviting me to be one of the team that writes

St. Stephen's Devotionals and rekindled my confidence as a writer. My thanks extend to the members of this Church who make me feel that I am loved and appreciated and have provided me with the opportunity to serve those who are in need.

Part 1
An Illusive Reality

Chapter 1
Inner Resources

Why blue pebbles? These colorful little stones inspired me to finally write this book after thinking about it for a very long time. I found them several years ago when a bright blue pebble about the size of a pea caught my attention when I was walking Heidi, my miniature schnauzer. Intrigued by its azure color, I pocketed the pretty little stone, took it home and deposited it on my dresser. The next day, I found two more pebbles flaunting their beauty against the dull brown earth and on the black tar of the little street where I walked; I added them to the others until they developed into a little blue pile. One or two each day appeared in unlikely places. After a rain I would discover them imbedded in mud. However, nothing deterred me; I extricated them and unloaded my odd collection onto my dresser when I returned home. The little blue pile grew unruly, and I dedicated a small mother of pearl box, a treasured gift, to be their container. I kept wondering where these incongruous pebbles came from and why they were blue.

I recognized that it was pretty weird of me to collect these little nuggets. The children in the neighborhood, noting my obsession, occasionally joined in my game and contributed any they found. I added these of lesser importance to my cache while being reluctant to tell the donors that a large part of my pleasure was in the discovery. The box was beginning to overflow when the source of pebbles dried up leaving my questions unanswered but not forgotten.

The children had invented explanations as to their origin, a factor not as important to me as understanding what the finding of them meant. I am a retired psychotherapist with a Jungian frame of reference, and I know something about symbolism and synchronicity, (meaningful coincidences that can't be explained in a cause-effect manner). I felt that my interest in and my attachment to those little stones had a meaning that lay hidden in my unconscious mind. I also knew how to go about retrieving that information. The message of the blue pebbles could emerge during meditation.

Before I got around to meditating on them, however, I awoke in the middle of the night and was unable to get back to sleep. This was a great time to ask my question because being close to the sleep state meant the contents of the unconscious would be more accessible than during the day. With intensity I asked the simple question, "What do the blue pebbles mean?" and instantly I received an intuitive message, "*Random acts of kindness.*"

Instinctively I fired back a rejection thinking that an answer from the unconscious mind would never be framed in day-to-day language. "That can't be right—it sounds like a bumper sticker!" I protested. However, my rejection was rejected.

IMPORTANT MESSAGE

FOR _____

DATE _____ TIME _____

M _____

OF _____

PHONE _____

☐ FAX   AREA   NUMBER   EXTENSION
☐ MOBILE

☐ PLEASE CALL	☐ WILL CALL AGAIN
☐ CAME TO SEE YOU	☐ WANTS TO SEE YOU
☐ RETURNED YOUR CALL	☐ URGENT

NOTE _____

_____

_____

_____

_____

_____ OPERATOR

BLIND INDUSTRIES
1-888-322-4567

NSN 7530-01-501-2688

The following answer is paraphrased:

"Acts of kindness can link everyone and everything into a meaningful, harmonious whole. Kindness is needed and is beneficial because every thing in the universe is linked. You may think everything is separate, but this is not true. Each individual, along with all of nature, is part of the totality. Kindness creates peace."

When I received that message I knew that my finite mind would never be able to appreciate the depth or completely understand that information, but I felt contented; I went back to sleep feeling satisfied and peaceful.

Excitement flooded me when I awoke the next morning and I called my son to tell him about my nocturnal adventure. He caught my excitement and quickly responded with his own intuitive understanding of the message. I was amazed that he would see anything different from what I had received, but I listened.

He said, "I'll tell you what I think it means. I think those stones you've been collecting are symbols of those dreams and weird happenings that you've been wanting to write about for so long."

My initial response was that he was projecting what he himself needed to hear. He is a singer-songwriter with a stack of his own songs and lyrics he has written over a lifetime and never recorded despite the urgings of those who have heard them and consider themselves his fans. Both of us were creative people who were stuck in terms of sharing our gift.

I also realized that both meanings had validity. This rang true to me, and I knew that symbols are never limited to one meaning; they are multi-faceted. In contrast, a sign means just what it says; "exit" means the way out, nothing more. You need to pay attention to your instinctive reaction to an expanded understanding. Does it feel right or does something tell you it doesn't fit? My son's interpretation felt right to me, and I decided to try once more to tell what I thought of as "my stories".

I remembered two fairly recent dreams that spoke to that very subject. My husband and I were attending church in a small town where we lived after retiring. The congregation was too sparse to have a choir, and the young woman who played the organ had to take time out to have a baby. No one else could play, which meant we would be without music. Church with no music was unacceptable to me; music helped evoke my spiritual feelings. Something drastic needed to be done.

I played the piano a little bit and knew chords, so I took it upon myself to play the organ. I thought that surely the similarity of the two instruments would make the transition feasible; however, something was lost in the translation. Not a service went by that I didn't make mistakes, and this upset me so much that a dream came along to soothe my feelings and help me forgive myself for being so imperfect.

I am standing directly behind an old American Indian woman who is instructing me. She is sitting cross-legged on a blanket, her long, gray hair streaming across her shoulders and down her back. She is holding an earthen bowl and she brings it close to her body. She then moves the bowl away from her body and holds it forth with outstretched arms, seemingly offering it to someone unseen. Intuitively

> I hear her message: "Gifts are not meant to be kept to oneself. Gifts are meant for sharing."

Just in case I didn't understand that meaning, another dream followed that same night:

> I am observing the inside of a large closet. Shelves run around the interior walls and various objects sit on those shelves. An overhead light is shining on them; however, I realize that the closet door is shut. I know that I should open that door.

Such dreams are not easily forgotten; they are far more important that the usual "house-keeping dreams" that bring our psyche back into balance at the end of a day. Dreams of this ilk are clearly meant as guidance and they have a profound impact on the dreamer.

Each object or person in a dream is meaningful. The old Indian woman is a crone, a wise old woman who advises me. Her hair symbolizes the ideas or wisdom that issue forth from her mind; it is long and gray, a way of saying she has lived many years. She offers me wisdom that has distilled out over a lifetime and is more significant than advice gleaned from any single, ordinary happening. The bowl was not fine porcelain, which would have been manufactured (man-made); it is made of clay—a blending of earth and water, the very essence of nature. Mother Earth provides the ground that supports and nourishes life; water is necessary to sustain life, and it is also a symbol of Spirit.

In the second dream, the objects on the shelves are talents or any small thing we can give or do for one another that connects us in a loving manner. These gifts can't be passed on to others while they are sitting on the shelf behind a closed closet door.

The organist returned, and I rejoined the congregation with a decided sense of relief. Life went on, and I was able to follow the dream guidance to some extent. I expressed my artistic ability through painting and wrote a mystery novel that was published; yet the book I really wanted to write kept rumbling around in my mind awaiting expression. These dreams joined the collection of other meaningful dreams and experiences that I had stashed away for future inclusion in "the book".

Paying attention to your dreams can provide guidance for living a fruitful life; they can function as an instrument to enhance the unfoldment of one's personality. Dreams that are not valued or understood remain an untapped resource throughout life. However, many people I've talked to are interested in dreams but complain that they can't remember them and don't know what they mean.

This book is intended to provide tools for remembering and ways to explore their meaning. I will use my own dreams because some of them were so clear that their message is easily discernable.

Dreams are not the only thing I write about; I have experienced several synchronistic events–those startling coincidences that can't be explained in terms of cause and effect. Some of these were so amazing that I would call them "peak experiences". These occurrences are rare and often written off as "weird" and ignored because of lack of understanding.

I believe this information that can be useful to others who are interested in delving into the meaning of this mysterious aspect of life. I have felt called upon to offer this information to others, yet how does one write about a subject so ephemeral? How does one effectively describe the nonmaterial?

Each blue pebbles tells a story that I experienced through a dream or synchronistic event. I believe that each has a message meant to be passed on to others as a gift of caring that can link us together in a loving, positive consciousness. None of these pebbles originated in my ego; I see them as gifts from Spirit. I hesitated to express this— somehow it seemed not right to try to change the ephemeral into matter. However, I also realized that one should not receive a gift without acknowledging and thanking the giver. I finally decided that if Spirit meant these gifts to be shared surely Spirit would help me complete this daunting task.

I had written bits and pieces of this previously, but I finally began my task in earnest. I gathered old journals and notes from the past, reviewed what they had to say and began writing. No book ever had a longer gestation period. I would write with messianic zeal for a while and then come to a screeching halt.

I couldn't explain what my dreams meant without revealing what had occurred in my life, and I dreaded that. People would see my imperfection! Horrors! Therefore, the writing proceeded bumpily until I had a dream in which I saw the book finished, its contents explained, symbolically illustrated, and actually being handed to a group of readers. But I am getting ahead of my story.

I have added a poem at the end of each chapter. Most of them were written at the time the dreams occurred. Just as each dream is a gift of Spirit so is a poem. A poem issues force from that mysterious inner dimension without trumpets to herald its arrival and deserves to be acknowledged and preserved.

To reap the benefits of any gift, one must be receptive. I invite you to lay aside your skepticism and explore the world of dreams and unusual happenings.

Dreams play a major role in this book because they have played an important role in my life. My interest in them focused during my early days as a mental health professional when I worked as a counselor at Family Service Center, Houston in the sixties. The staff received in-service training as a part of its continuing education program, and Dr. Kenneth Beach, a Jungian analyst, taught us how to work with dreams. I soon discovered that I had a better than average intuitive understanding of the language of dreams. Jung's viewpoint made sense to me, and I began attending a weekly Jung study group to supplement my knowledge of his work.

What do these mysterious nocturnal dramas have to say that might benefit our lives? The simplest answer is that some dreams appear to perform a "house-keeping" role for the psyche. After a day filled with unresolved issues and tension, dreams come along to put the psyche back in balance. For example, a dream could help us resolve the anger that couldn't be expressed at an unfair boss and help us be able to return to a more normal state of being in order to go undaunted to the office the next morning. On another occasion, we may experience feelings of lust that need to be ignored. For instance, one might encounter an attractive, but off-limits, member of the opposite sex when it would be highly inappropriate to act on our impulses. That feeling must be shoved aside to land unceremoniously in the unconscious mind and provide the fodder for the coming night's dreams.

When dreams aren't able, for some reason, to bring the psyche back into balance, the material that lies in the unconscious can become like a splinter buried deep in one's finger; it can fester and cause problems. When a person is uncomfortable enough to seek help from a psychotherapist, dreams can serve as a bridge between conscious and unconscious mind, helping the therapist to access the problem that needs to be addressed in treatment.

All of the contents of the unconscious aren't negative, however. Answers to problems, creative ideas, forgotten information, even unheeded signs of danger may exist there awaiting discovery. The most important aspect is that spiritual feelings arrive through this channel. If we honor and listen to dreams, and learn to read the language of symbolism, we can discover an invaluable inner resource.

Perhaps the most familiar type of dream that the average person remembers is the anxiety dream; it is common to everyone. An individual's imagery may be similar over their lifetime having to do with previous experiences when they felt unsure of themselves. Some people try to fly and can't get off the ground, some walk through sand with great difficulty; some are in danger of falling. Some dream of appearing naked in front of a crowd.

The night before I was to register for the first time at the University of Texas, my anxiety about that task caused me to have a nightmare. I was clinging high up on the exterior of the University tower grasping a screened window like those found on houses in the days when windows were kept open because we didn't have air conditioning. They were flimsy to say the least. An anxiety dream may be frightening, but somehow it helps relieve or diminishes the anxiety. Maybe it just says—that's how bad it was and you survived.

Several years after I graduated and went to work in my chosen profession, when I had anxiety I would have a dream related to school. I would be trying to find some classroom, forgetting my assignment, losing my textbooks or not having an assignment completed. After I had been working for a while, I would dream of not being able to find my office or remember the phone number for my answering service. After retirement, any time that I am not taking charge of my life, I may dream of not being able to control my car, at times even sliding downhill or not being able to steer around a corner.

Let me share with you a short dream of mine that is easy to read; it occurred when I was still new to the counseling profession.

> I see a stage; it seems to be the outdoor theater at Herman Park. It is lit and a performance is about to take place. I know I am supposed to go on stage, but I am not there. I am in the prop storage room located directly under the stage. I am hiding behind a screen that is part of the scenery stored there.

Need I say more? How more succinctly could the apprehension of a neophyte counselor be described? Anyone with any sensibility would be concerned about what they are called upon to do. I spoke to my supervisor about my fear of saying the wrong thing and causing the client pain or exacerbating their problem. With the wisdom that arises from experience she replied, "Don't worry about that; if you say something they shouldn't hear, it will go in one ear and out the other. Their defenses won't allow them to hear it."

Another example of a dream that functioned to relieve anxiety occurred when I led my first therapy group. Fairly soon after I had started working at the Family Service Center in Houston I was to co-lead a therapy group. The group came into being because I noticed a particular need when I was doing my weekly turn at taking telephone calls requesting our services. Callers would be screened for appropriateness and either given an in-take appointment or were referred to a more suitable agency or provider. I noticed that we were getting an inordinate amount of calls from young women who were having what we called an identity crisis. These very young adults had come to work in the big city of Houston and now found themselves alone and deprived of supportive families and friends; they were feeling a lot of anxiety. I sent out requests to counselors on staff and asked if they had any similar clients whom they thought could profit from group therapy.

This would be my first experience in leading such a group and I knew I'd need help. A young woman offered to co-lead; the only problem was that neither of us was experienced, but we had supervision. The response to our request for potential group members was so large that several had to be rejected as candidates. We ended up with a group of eight which was the limit of what we thought we could handle.

The date was set. Our supervisor said that the first night would be hard; they probably would be reluctant to talk, and we would have to draw them out to get started. We knew that members of a group think of themselves as "I" until, at some time in the future, they begin to refer to the group as "we". Only then would it be cohesive and become really effective.

The members gathered that first night and looked at each other timorously for a only few minutes before they began eagerly reaching out to one another. Everyone started talking at once. I felt like I was trapped inside a popcorn popper. I tried desperately to get control, and it seemed to me that co-leader Jane curled up in a corner and died.

Once the meeting ended and our group dispersed, Jane unloaded on me for talking too much, and I was angry with her for not supporting me. Each of us went home exhausted and feeling overwhelmed. The following dream came to my rescue to "fix" me that night:

> Scene 1. I am standing in a place that must be a train station because I see several people boarding a train. The train pulls out of the station. Horrors! It's leaving without me!
>
> Scene 2. I am running at break-neck speed alongside the railroad track. My footing is precarious; I am running on gravel and it slopes downward from the rails. I am running so fast that I can see my knees rising as I plunge ahead disregarding the danger of falling. I am desperate. I need to get to the next station before that train arrives. I need to get on board. I am supposed to be leading that train!

No one could read that dream and not understand what it is saying, however, it can be read at a deeper depth than the function of addressing my immediate anxiety. Trains in those days were something one took when going a long distance; they were serious business. This train trip could represent my journey through life, and the passengers on board could be seen as different aspects of my personality.

That person who is me had been doggedly going ahead in life, setting goals and reaching them, but something had occurred that jarred me into the realization that I was not in control of my life! In the outer world, I had survived the tragic failure of a marriage, gotten a college education later in life than most, learned to live alone and take care of my day-to-day needs, but in the truest sense of the word, I did not know who I was. I wasn't too far removed from being the obedient child or the compliant wife or dedicated mother. I was also the product of the age in which I lived; women were supposed to be at home having children—not entering the work force. Talk about identity crisis!

In the truest sense, I wasn't centered and in charge of my life; my security lay in my adopted role of therapist. The fact that I had married again meant I had someone to "take care of me", and I was oblivious to the fact that I was taking care of everyone but myself. Strangely enough, I wasn't far different from those young group members who at this point in their lives were feeling lost. I came to realize as time went on that clients often came to us so that we could learn from one another even if I was the one labeled the counselor.

Because of my own life experience I was able to empathize with those clients and empathy is an important ingredient of being an effective counselor; I had the education and the life-experience that enabled me to perform effectively. Of course it is essential that, as a counselor, I didn't operate out of my weakness rather than out of my strength. Counselors should in turn see someone who will help them become as centered as they are capable of being.

The real healing factor in my relationship with clients lay in the fact that I came to see their true being rather that the facade they presented to the world, and I came to love that person despite the inevitable flaws each of us has. When counseling is successful the scars, freckles and warts fade into oblivion to reveal the real person with whom you are working, and that person is okay. Everyone needs that, and therefore I profited from the relationship as well as the client. We learned from each other.

Counseling is terminated when the client can walk out having recognized that he or she can get along in this world and cope with the vicissitudes of life without the counselor. The last step is termination when they can leave knowing that they can live in this world and manage their lives themselves—not flawlessly, but feeling more centered, capable of making decisions, and dealing with the inevitable rough spots that occur on their journey. Today we might describe them as people who "feel comfortable in their own skin".

Teaching clients to work with their dreams could help them understand who they really were and where they were on their life journey. Using the same techniques would help me become more centered and have a more strong sense of self. Change is ironically a permanent part of our life's unfoldment. Our task is to bring forth the God-given potential of our personality, and dreams are a precious tool in this adventure. Come join me to learn how to do it.

DREAMS

In the dark of night
the stage is lit
in the labyrinth
of my mind,
the drama unfolds.
Enter characters
who act out my myths,
encapsulate in one brief scene,
or more,
a myriad of meanings
that slip too soon
from memory,
like changing cloud forms.
I seize them tightly,
risk reshaping them
into lost meaning.

Does honor impress you,
metaphor of space
and timelessness?
If so, speak to me.
Come forth to meet the light.
My meager words
attempt to pay you homage,
my finite mind
seeks to know your Knowing.

Chapter 2
The Importance
Of Dreams

This book is not written to cover the history of dreams, to present a scientific explanation of why we dream, or even a guaranteed method of flawless interpretation. It is meant to show you to how to work with your dreams and I will be using my own dreams to illustrate. They are available because I have kept a dream journal almost my entire adult life, and because these dreams are easily understood. In addition to having been taught by a Jungian analyst, I attended a weekly Jung study group and went to various dream workshops over the years.

In the book I also include synchronistic events—those highly unusual occurrences that can't be explained in terms of cause and effect. These happenings speak of the presence of a Higher Source that is active in our lives and that can furnish guidance through meditation. Because of these experiences, and because of the wisdom I recognized in dreams, I began to feel a need to share this material. Many people are curious about dreams, but frustrated because they don't know how to discern their meaning. Others think that dreams have no meaning at all, and regard synchronicity as happenstance. Some people have never acknowledged an intuitive thought, and if they have had one they labeled it a hunch and credited their ego with having manifested it.

Human beings throughout the ages have been interested in their dreams. We know that many primitive tribes thought their dreams were evidence of another life that they lived at night. They looked upon this dream-life as very real and thought that dreams provided guidance for the life lived during the day.

Most of us are aware of at least two of the literally thousands of dreams recounted in the Hebrew Torah and the Christian Bible. One is the dream of Jacob's ladder and the other tells of an Egyptian pharaoh's dream that Joseph was called upon to explain. Joseph interpreted the dream successfully, and the grateful pharaoh elevated him to a position of power in Egypt that eventually led to the captive Israelite's exodus from Egypt.

Much later in history, medical doctors started studying and treating the mentally ill, and the specialization of psychiatry came into existence. Exploring the patient's dreams was found to provide a helpful treatment tool. Freud was the first of these psychiatrists to become prominent in this field. He wrote a classic book about dreams. He thought the unconscious mind was filled with unacceptable instincts, desires and personal memories, and that dreams were a way of disguising the hidden wishes of the dreamer, primarily of a sexual nature. He believed that dream symbols led away from the problem.

Carl Jung studied under Sigmund Freud, but eventually differed with him, and they went their separate ways. Freud resented Jung's separation, and Jung became alienated from him and his followers as a result. As time went on Jung became more and more recognized, and other psychiatrist presented their versions of the meaning of dreams, but Freud had won his position as pioneer in the profession.

Both Freud and Jung drew their conclusions about dreams from vast clinical experience. Carl Jung studied 65,000 dreams before espousing his dream theory. His break with Freud came because of a disagreement over the contents of the unconscious. Jung did not think that dreams functioned to hide meaning; he believed they stored personal memories, instincts and altruistic thoughts. Freud was an atheist while Jung believed in God and that spiritual thoughts as well as creativity issued forth from the unconscious mind.

Carl Jung drew on the intuitive nature of the right hemisphere of the brain. Jung's unique contribution to the study of psychiatry was in describing another, deeper layer of consciousness that he called an archetypal layer or the "collective unconscious"; he saw it as universal, inborn and containing "patterns of instinctual behavior". One example of this would be the fact that Eskimos may dream of snakes, but have never seen one. Jung wrote volumes about this, but since I am not a Jungian analyst, I will simply give you an overview of the expansiveness of Jung's viewpoint as well as the depth of his understanding.

One of Jung's concepts that was important to me was the "feminine and the masculine principles". The feminine principle is similar to what was later discovered to be the function of the right hemisphere of the brain and it describes a type of energy characterized by the intuitive, feeling, nurturing and receptive nature. It is interesting to note that this is similar to the Yin of ancient Eastern philosophy that is also associated with the moon and the dark of night.

In contrast to the feminine principle, Jung's described the masculine principle as an outward thrusting energy expressed by the intellect, reason, logic, and "the word"; this is descriptive of the left hemisphere of the brain. This can be seen as corresponding to the Eastern Yang, which is also associated with the brightness of the sun. It is interesting to realize that this ancient civilization, sans the scientific method, described the function of the right and the left hemispheres of the brain which function in opposite ways as they take in and process information.

Another way to look at this dichotomy is that the "left-brain" uses deductive reasoning. It moves forward from the unknown toward a goal in a step-by-step manner; it is a logical, reasonable way of using what is tangible and measurable. The scientific method is based on a cause and effect relationship between what it observes. This is a valuable way of thinking but not the only way; the original impulse that caused the scientist to decide to do a certain research project would have emerged from the right-brain, a fact often overlooked. Another difference in the ways the hemispheres function is that the right does not see things in bits and pieces as does the left; it sees a whole picture taking in ambiguities and opposites and compares through the use of metaphors.

The right hemisphere intuits an answer given only some of the component parts. The intuitive response can be wrong, and its offerings should always be checked out with reason. It is apparent why intuition is often distrusted, but it shouldn't be disregarded. Ironically, the marriage of these opposite is required for creativity. Discounting intuition ignores part of the creative process.

The important thing about the brain is that everyone has two hemispheres and uses both in varying degrees. One hemisphere is dominant; right-handed people have a left dominance, left-handed have a dominant right because of a biological crossover.

Again, it isn't an "either or" proposition but a combination of resources rather than operating totally from one hemisphere or the other. Part of our psychological growth over time is to get in touch with the aspects of self that are not dominant.

Most commonly we see men getting more in touch with their intuitive, feeling nature as they mature, while women may become more assertive. All of this is highly affected by culture. Today's young women are much freer to be assertive than in my day. Rosie the riveter of the Second World War expresses the beginning of that change. These patterns can be understood when one thinks of how roles relate to the demands made of different sexes; primitive man went out into the environment to obtain food for his family often encountering wild animals while seeking his prey. Women bore and nurtured the children, hunted and gathered, but that was a less dangerous task and called upon their intuitive instincts.

It is also understandable that the scientific revolution and industrialization brought about a respect for the scientific method that has led to the degradation of intuition. People have been frightened by intuitive extremes that can cause trouble and lead people to believe unreasonable things and behave in what may seem to others ridiculous ways.

I am not left-handed and don't have a dominant right brain, but it is certainly very active and highly affects my view of life. I came from a hard working, practical family but my maternal side included artists and my father's family was musical. These weren't hobbies; they were serious interests. As an adult, I found myself living in a world in which my view of reality often seemed different. I kept encountering circumstances where my experiences and beliefs were questioned or discounted.

This caused me to become more and more aware of what many other people were evidently missing. This inspired me to tell "my side of the story", and this book is the result. Let me help you discover what remembering and understanding the meaning of your dreams can contribute to your life. Let me point out and perhaps help you recognize those weird things that happen that can't be explained logically. Life is a marvelous mystery painted in brilliant color; it was never meant to be seen in black and white.

Now that we have a little background on the early psychological studies of dreams, let's consider how to go about understanding them. It can be difficult to take them seriously because they seem to be ridiculous and sometimes embarrassing. They present an unvarnished truth about our personality and what is happening in our life that is sometimes hard to face for they are always blatantly honest. The solution to this is to learn to laugh at these aspects of self. This is the reason one must not only suspend disbelief but also put aside a judgmental attitude before trying to discern their meaning. If you try to examine a dream from a critical point of view, it will simply disappear into the dark recesses of the mind and hide there. Accept its craziness and its honesty, or forget about reaping any profit from what it has to offer.

A dream can be described as a nocturnal event of visual imagery. It can be viewed as a story told in metaphorical form, and it is couched in symbolism, the language of the unconscious mind, Therefore the first puzzle to confront in studying dreams is that symbolism. How does one understand its meaning? First, realize that a symbol is different from a sign. A symbol has more than one meaning; in fact, it may have multiple facets while a sign means one thing. For instance, an Exit sign says this is a way out but it doesn't say it is a locked or unlocked door, or one of several other possible pieces of information.

I don't suggest that you buy a book on symbols from the checkout counter of the local super market; the information may lead you astray. Of first importance is that anything written on symbols that doesn't stress that the definitions are very individually generated, is completely off base. The book, "Man and His Symbols", by Carl Jung and his associates, is the best place to start, and there are others written from serious research. Jung suggested that one should learn as much as possible about symbols, and then forget it when working with dreams. I believe this means one should not let information from a book control your interpretation. What you read should be digested and then allowed to drop into the unconscious to give one's intuition a chance to express its wisdom through the interpretation.

Symbols are always personal and evolve out of an individual's knowledge and experience. They can mean contradictory things and you must consider how one operates in your particular dream. An apple may be a delicious fruit, but to someone who once bit into one expecting to find a juicy, crisp, tasty tidbit and found a worm, an apple may be the last thing chosen by the unconscious as a positive symbol. The fairy tale of Snow White includes a poisoned apple and that could even serve as a symbol of hidden danger, but an "apple for the teacher" carries positive meaning. What feels right to you?

A helpful way to understand a symbol is to meditate on it and imagine actually becoming that symbol; then, describe yourself. This is always the very essence of its qualities. The meaning must fit in with the dream story, and this can only be verified through an intuitive feeling of comfort or one of "no-ness".

In dream labs during the 1950s, thousands of volunteers were monitored during sleep so that researchers could study dreams. They found that dreams occur in the fourth stage of dreaming when the rapid eye movement, or REM stage, was observed. Dreams occur about forty minutes after going to sleep, and we have 5 to 7 dreams a night. The last one may be forty to forty five minutes long. During our lifetime we may spend seven years dreaming. That should tell us that dreams have a decided function in one's life.

If you think you do not dream, forget that. Everyone dreams. Some people simply do not remember them. Introspective people such as myself may dream in long, elaborate sequences. I think of these changes as different scenes within the dream. Extraverts usually dream short ones.

Dream research tells us all dreams are in color though many don't remember that aspect. In my own experience, I tend to remember color when the dream is more important than usual. When I am awakened in the middle of a dream I may remember color.

If you want to remember your dreams, send an emphatic message to your dream maker before going to sleep that you will remember your dreams in the morning. Keep some paper and a pencil beside your bed for instant recording. If you get up in the middle of the night, record a word or two; it may help you remember the dream the next morning.

Ideally, you should lie still when you awaken and review the dream before arising because even a small movement can send it flying; then record it. The position or placement of people or objects can contribute to understanding; therefore it is helpful to draw diagrams, blueprints, and any detail that could be important.

I like to buy an attractive notebook to serve as my journal; I prefer one with a cover that is simple in decoration and in a color I like. It will be a spiral one with a back sturdy enough to give my paper support while I writing sitting in my chair. Be sure and date the dreams of each night so that you can go back later and see how they relate to what was going on in your life at the time. It is for this reason that I combine my dreams with ordinary journal entries. I mark dreams that I feel are of special importance with a yellow marker so that I can refer to them easily. When your book is filled, label the cover with dates to facilitate possible future reference.

The feeling tone you are left with when you awaken is perhaps the most important thing to recognize about a dream. Is it frightening, sad, happy, or satisfying? What has happened in the twenty-four hours prior to the dream?

That may explain what triggered it, but another meaning may lie deeper.

Consider the objects in the dream; are they man-made or a part of nature? Do they reflect something currently occurring in your life or do they belong to the past? Like a three act play dreams often are about something you are dealing with at the moment. They show you the problem, how you are handling it, and where it will go if you keep doing the same thing. Sometimes they offer a solution.

Dreams occasionally can be about the future. My own grandmother was well known in her family for having had some pre-cognitive dreams. The most memorable one to me occurred when she was a young wife living in Mississippi. One morning before breakfast she told of dreaming about the body of a dead black man in water with his hair entangled in the reeds. In her words, she told me, "I was pregnant at the time, and in those days we didn't go outside when we were 'showing'; however, I saw a neighbor running across the field, and I stepped out of the screened door and called to ask him what was happening. He told me they had found a body in the creek, and described it exactly like I had seen it in my dream."

Years later my grandfather died and she moved the family to Texas to be near her sister. Every now and then she would receive a check from Mr. Fox, the partner of the mercantile store my grandfather had owned with him. Some customer would have come in and paid a bill he owed and Mr. Fox would send my grandmother her share.

One morning she announced to the family that she had dreamed that Mr. Fox had sent a check and that it was colored blue instead of the usual yellow. That day the check arrived and it was blue as she had described. Neither time nor space are dimensions recognized in dreams.

Quite a while before I moved to Wimberley, Texas three years ago, I had a dream that showed what I knew was my car, but is was a dark color in contrast to the beige one I was driving at the time. Oil paintings I had done were inexplicably adorning the interior! At the time I had that dream I didn't know what it meant. I assumed the dream had to do with a move of some kind since a car is often the symbol of your "vehicle through life", but I couldn't understand why the color was dark. Later on we traded my car for similar one with much less mileage, and it was such a dark green that it looked almost black. The paintings were a symbol of the one thing I would always take with me—my creative talent.

Another dream that cannot be explained in terms of the outer reality was one that occurred when my cousin Sue had died. I was talking to my mother on the phone while arranging to rendezvous with her at the Houston airport to fly to Lubbock for the funeral. I said, "Sue told me when I talked to her not to worry about her going on; she was ready to do that." Mother was startled by this statement and asked when I had talked to her. It was then that I realized that I had not talked her but had received that information in a dream.

Another cousin, Charles, was lost when his plane went down in the Pacific Ocean during World War II. And for years I dreamt of searching for him in foreign countries—occasionally thinking I had gotten a glimpse of his face. I finally dreamt of finding him. He invited me to join him, but I declined, saying I needed to stay there because another cousin, Ralph, was coming to visit and I needed to be there for him. They never found any trace of the plane Charles was in; if we had been able to get closure on that death by having a body, I probably would not have had those dreams. My sleeping mind simply kept trying to solve the puzzle so that I could get on with my life. Charles was the nearest thing I had to a brother.

Years earlier I had a dream that pictured a tree like the one at the front of my property where I lived at that time; it was an ancient, huge oak that I loved. The tree in my dream was planted in sand and it fell to the ground. I awoke greatly distressed and had no idea what it meant. I only understood that it was some kind of major loss. I think of a tree as meaning "the tree of life" (something very personal), and whatever it meant appeared to be stable but actually wasn't because it was rooted in sand. This one simple scene turned out to have a lot of meaning. That gorgeous old oak was later struck by lightening and toppled during a storm. Later than that, the marriage I had thought so perfect failed, and my married name at that time was Sands.

I did find the mention of trees falling in some professional's interpretation of a dream. A tree that fell in a forest could symbolize clearing space in the forest to allow information from the unconscious (the forest) to come into the conscious mind. That interpretation was not threatening so I latched onto it and ignored the fact that my dream-tree wasn't in a forest. That meaning was less foreboding, and I did not foresee the breakup of the marriage. It is interesting to note when I look back on it that the break-up involved a significant change in my consciousness. At the time we had fit together more easily because he was an atheist and I was a "temporary agnostic".

Characters who appear in your dreams present another puzzle. A person in your dream may be that person, but is more likely to be an aspect of yourself that is similar to that individual. If it is Sally whom you knew in the fourth grade, it probably represents the Sally part of your personality. How would you describe her?

One way to discover the metaphor represented by the dream is to compose a sentence or paragraph that tells the story of the dream. "This is a story about__," (fill in the blank).

Dream study groups are helpful. Meet with a few people who are interested and willing to openly discuss private matters. Each person should agree that what is said in the group stays in the group. One member reports a dream. Then one by one the other group members tell what it means to them while the dreamer remains silent. The feedback is always useful. Remember, the important thing is that only the dreamer can tell whether an interpretation rings true, and that means listening to one's inner guidance that arrives through intuition. Even if you don't discover a dream's meaning, just paying attention to it is helpful.

One way to look at our self is to think of our ego as the CEO of our life that deals with the outer reality. What we regard as "I" is actually a limited concept of self; it is but a small part of who we actually are. "The tip of an iceberg" is a much-used symbol to describe the ego because so much of us lies outside our conscious awareness. Our intuition tells us there is something more to life than what we know, and we have an innate desire to search for that meaning.

This wholeness of Self is often spelled with a capital letter in contrast to the ego self, which is spelled with a lower case letter. Higher Self includes our connection with Divine Mind—our soul. The unfoldment of our personality occurs as we mature and more of our innate potential emerges. We become more of who we were intended to be.

Just paying attention to your dreams is thought to strengthen the axis of ego self to Self, which contributes to wholeness and good mental health. Dreams are more likely to be remembered when the connection between your conscious mind and the unconscious, where dreams originate, is honored.

The following are some specific suggestions for the process:

1. Record the entire dream, noting feelings, dialogue, and watch for a theme or story it portrays. Dream images are always symbolic pictures that portray something about yourself or your life situation.

2. If you dream of a person it is probably a symbol of a part of your own personality—an aspect of self you ignore or don't like, and thus a non-judgmental attitude is essential.

3. Symbols can often be understood if you simply define them. If it is a place, do you have some association with it? It may help to describe it.

4. Consider whether an object is man-made or part of nature. Man-made imagery such as buildings or vehicles represent acquired states of mind or ways of acting. Animals, plants and scenery are part of nature and therefore can show instincts or emotions.

5. Numbers, forms, and colors show patterns of balance revolution For instance 3 is a "moving number" whereas 4 is balanced. The shape of a circle denotes

wholeness, eternity, or Spirit. Examples of color are the blue that depicts sadness or wisdom, red would be a more aggressive or active color, green could depict growth, etc.

6. Dreams may use word play such as puns, slang phrases, or slips of the tongue. The action in the dream may be represented by any of these. I once dreamed of sliding a tray around the cafeteria runway to place food and I had to negotiate a corner. In the dream this represented turning a corner in my life.

7. A dream may depict a conflict between different aspects of your personality. For instance, part of you may want to do one thing, another part may disagree. Just listening to a dialogue between these opposites should help resolve the problem.

If you study a symbol in your dream and don't get a sense of understanding, you may be blocking on some aspect of your personality. It may be something learned as a "shouldn't" in childhood that is an inappropriate way of being in adulthood. If you feel uncomfortable or disapproving toward an image, it's probably an aspect of your shadow—that part of yourself that lies outside your conscious awareness. It's wise to face it even you don't want to do so. Everything has its good and its bad; you may free up potential for growth. An interesting thing about the shadow is that you don't see it yourself, but other people can see it.

Years ago when I first started studying dreams, I read a statement by Dr. Montague Ulman who at that time was Director of the Sleep Research Lab at Miamedes Hospital in New York: "Dreams are our most untapped natural resource, metaphorical vignettes that, when explored, can help reveal emotions we have about all aspects of life. They have incredible potential for healing and restoring the psyche; in fact, some dream specialists speculate that the real purpose of dreaming may be to heal us emotionally."

Another resource I used at that time was Morton Kelsey, an Episcopal priest and Jungian analyst. In his book, Dreams: a Way to Listen to God, he states, "The dream may be one of the most common avenues through which God reaches out to us. Dreams should be taken very seriously."

Dreams need to be addressed in an adult manner. They can be dangerous because they can play tricks on you; remember that intuitive answers can by incorrect and should always be checked by the left-brain function of logical thinking. However, dreams do tell us something about ourselves, situations, and other people that we haven't recognized.

Having said that, I will tell you that the dreams that inspired the writing of this book were of a spiritual nature, and they were clustered in a series that occurred over succeeding nights. They reawakened my faith in a Higher Power after some fifteen years I spent lost in the desert of agnosticism after a painful divorce. Revelatory dreams are rare, but these broke through the barriers of my disbelief to deliver messages of Truth. It was definitely my individual Truth, yet I believe that those dreams also included a universal message of a creative force that far exceeds the limitations of the personal ego. Each of us has an innate desire to seek and find something far more fulfilling than what we know as our self; in this book I will share with you the dreams that opened the door of an inner awakening for me that enhanced my life.

The non-rational can never be measured or described by cause and effect, yet it can be valuable beyond words in terms of one's "beingness". Learn to appreciate your dreams and understand what they are saying at least to some extent, and you can discover who you really are. I invite you to open that door.

IN SEARCH OF TRUTH

In search of Truth
I go,
lamp in hand
to light the corridors
of darkness.
I can't foretell
the right
or wrong direction.
Not all my turnings
will lead home,
nor all my paths
be smooth ones,
but if Truth does
indeed exist,
I know that
Truth will find me.

Chapter 3
Who I Am

Am I somehow different because the contents of my dreams have been so available to me, so lengthy, and often so easy to read? Not really. However, it may have something to do with my inherited, musical and creative bent that means my right brain is very active. It may also be related to the fact that my early years were spent in a loving, accepting environment. I grew up expecting the world to love and value me therefore I had little need to have a guarded attitude toward life. No life goes unchallenged, but for the most part mine was truly blessed.

I am no longer young and this book covers material gleaned from my entire life; the actual writing has been in process for several years. This entitles me to address you from the pedestal of my old age, but that very fact allows you to see a ribbon of events that string out over a lifetime. The only way to present this material to you is to use my life for a framework on which to display my stories, and this means personal exposure that I deplore but can't avoid.

I know full well that standing on pedestals displays one's clay feet to the world, but I've noticed that viewers find the sight of other people's clay feet to be comforting since they are often aware of their own, even though they may go to great length to hide them. At least this tells them that they are not alone. I also know that if I let you come too close, you will see up my skirt, and who wants to show their underpinnings to the world? However, no gift can be appreciated until one removes the wrapping paper and discards the decorative ribbon. I have to let you know who I am.

I am an only child born on April 6, 1925 exactly 9 months and twenty days after my young parents were married. They had just graduated from the only high school in Austin, Texas, then a small town despite being the state capitol. My parent's marriage culminated from a short courtship and I was, no doubt, created in passionate love. My mother had fallen madly in love with my father after seeing him and his older brother play a xylophone duet at an assembly program. The marriage and ensuing pregnancy surprised no one since these were pre-pill days.

College for either of my parents was never a consideration. Not many people went to the college in those days, and they were both the youngest children of large families and the money wasn't available. My dad had already been a professional musician for several years and once admitted to me that he had slept through many classes because of having played at dances with the family orchestra the previous night. He only had a public school education, but he was described as "always having his nose in a book".

After marriage my father began looking for more stable work that would provide for his little family. Finding a job that paid well and would give him more quality time at home was a daunting task since these were also the days of the Great Depression. Out of necessity, the young couple nestled into my grandmother's home along with my two maiden aunts who lived there with her.

My entry into the world occurred in Austin's Seaton Infirmary. The delivery was complicated by an umbilical cord wrapped precariously around my neck. This must have made my safe arrival doubly appreciated.

The mothering role was well known to my grandmother, and I quickly became the baby my aunts were fated never to have. My father had already been welcomed into the family as the prized addition of a much-needed titular male head of the household. Surely, I had entered the best possible world, and I also enjoyed the privilege of being the first female grandchild in my mother's family who lived in Austin and the very first grandchild in my father's.

My mother was artistic in many ways. She was noted for having begun sewing clothes for the family when she was so small that she had to stand to reach the peddle on the sewing machine. By the time I was old enough to notice, I realized that my mother's tailoring was impeccable, and she could sew anything I designed and we for which the money could be found to pay for the material.

My grandmother was a fine artist and her beautiful oil paintings hung in ours and in other homes. She had learned to paint at Oxford Women's College, which later became Mississippi State University. Her attendance was made possible by a small inheritance, and her sister also attended, learning and later teaching music. My mother also painted, and I discovered while looking in her class yearbook that she had been named the class poet of her high school.

One of my father's outstanding traits was his ability to relate to children at their level. They discovered in him another child. His arrival home from work always meant a great adventure lay in store for me. I would instruct my mother to tell him that I had flown away in my imaginary airplane, and I would gleefully squirm under the bed to hide in the darkness among an occasional dust bunny while he searched the house for me, loudly calling my name. My giggles would finally betray me and I would be dragged out of my hiding place to break free and chase around the house with him in pursuit. Life was one big playground to us during those early years, and I was his undisputed princess.

He was tall, slim and handsome in my eyes. All of his life people found him attractive and he had many friends. His family lived in Austin and was close. His father was a linotype operator who poured hot lead into forms that created the letters that produced newspapers. My paternal grandmother was a well-trained musician who taught each of her children various instruments. They formed the Pharr Family Orchestra and played at "all the dances until swing came in" according to my father.

Life for my mother's family was faced with little humor. My grandfather had died of typhoid fever when mother was four days old, leaving her mother with 6 children to raise at a time when women's place was in the home rather than the market place. Life was a serious matter for them, and my mother's early childhood was greatly affected by the circumstances surrounding her birth and early childhood.

After my grandfather's death, the family moved from their home in verdant Mississippi to live close to her sister in the hot, dusty West Texas town of Snyder. She supported the family by serving as the local Post Mistress. Later they moved to Austin where my grandmother worked in the State Legislature. By the time I joined them, the older offspring had left, and she had been able to retire. My aunts lived at home and were employed in State jobs, and we lived together in my grandmother's small frame house on Ruiz Street, relatively secure compared to countless others who were struggling to survive.

M'gran, my name for my grandmother, was tiny. When I was in the second grade, we moved away from Austin because of my father's work, but each time we returned I would run through the house to find her and bury myself in her soft body, my face pressed against the perfectly ironed apron she wore over her dress.

She was the consummate lady and remained bright and well-informed all of her days. Her delicate stature disguised her strength. She never was hurtful or spoke ill of anyone but was unyielding in her standards. Each day she arose before dawn and to have the house in order in case a neighbor came to visit, and it was always left in fairly good shape each night in case someone got sick and the doctor might have to be called.

I loved both of my aunts, but Charlotte was my favorite. She was my goddess—beautiful and popular, more fun than anyone else, and she adored me. As an older sister, Charlotte was assigned the task of watching over my mother to help my burdened grandmother; thus Mother and Charlotte were always close.

The other aunt, Ella Mae, was deeply affected by the
trauma of her early childhood—the loss of her father
followed by the drastic change in her environment. She hid
her insecure feelings by trying to impress people with her
brightness; however, she admitted to me late in her life that
she always felt less intelligent than her very bright siblings
and her mother. I had always suspected that her need to
be right must have arisen from a lack of confidence. She
worked too hard to prove her self worth, but it overlay a
sense of inferiority. She worked hard, was conscientious,
a good-hearted person and very generous but rather
controlling; I saw her as too pleased at discovering other
people's faults or mistakes. Poor Ellie, she wasn't as easy to
love as Charlotte whom I remember as an unlimited source
of unconditional love.

My father finally got a job as a surveyor, which meant
our little family had to move away from Austin for a while
and leave that loving support system. I was still in diapers
when my mother became ill with a bad cold caught while
hanging out wet diapers in freezing weather. My father's
work meant he was away from home most of the time,
which meant mother had no help in caring for me. No
antibiotics existed at that time, and she was diagnosed with
a "suspected case" of tuberculosis. The only prescribed
treatment was bed rest, and she was sent to a sanatorium
to recuperate, thus I "lost" both parents. In my little world,
my father disappeared and then my mother after I had
already been separated from my grandmother and aunts.

I was never deprived of caring love, however. My
mother's oldest sister eagerly came to the rescue and I went
to live with her family in Lubbock, Texas. She had lost
a baby girl who died when she was only a month or so

old. Having that baby live and slowly pass away was heart breaking, but she had another daughter a few years later who was of school age when I came to stay. "Aunt Sister", as I knew her, welcomed me into her arms and into her family, and my father visited when he was able.

My aunt tried valiantly to keep my mother informed of every detail of my budding life by writing letters to fill the missing pictures of that precious time of separation. One story handed down from that particular period was of my uncle playing his fiddle. He purposely played a "sour note" whereupon I would toddle over and pull on his pants leg until he stopped. The family was quick to recognize any sign of musical talent on my part, of course, and I did come to love music and thought of myself as a musician for years until my life path led in a different direction.

A crisis occurred when I was living with my aunt; I became seriously ill with scarlet fever, and the accompanying raging fever caused my hair to fall out. This was no small event since I had been blessed with a head full of curls. These were highly valued in pre-permanent days, and my family was dismayed when those pitiful little disconnected curls appeared on my hot pillow. My aunt regretfully gathered those little ringlets and stored them in a small box that I have to this day. It was incongruously covered in Christmas paper decorated with holly leaves and bright red berries, as if this colorful container could negate the tragedy of those forlorn curls and the memory of my bleak walk through the valley of death.

Once they were reassured that I would survive, the vigil began; when would my hair return? More importantly— would it again be curly? I lived with that shiny noggin for a long time. My grieving family disguised it with baby bonnets that I wore. By this time I was old enough to protest mightily over one of those bonnets. The family members repeated the story by imitating me wailing loudly, "I don't want to wear that one! That isn't peach, that is orange and I don't like orange!" Thus spoke the young artist.

Over future years of recording my dreams, hair appeared again and again—always symbolizing my thoughts or beliefs—something that issued forth from my head. For years it was never quite ready to be seen by the public; it was wet or too long or too short—a symbol of distrust in my ability to effectively express my belief system.

My absence of loved ones and my illness occurred at a very vulnerable stage in my life and left some psychological scars buried deep in my unconscious mind, outside of my awareness. At that age I believed, like any child, that I was the center of my universe. A baby cries when hungry and someone brings a bottle or mother provides a breast, one's wetness brings a dry diaper; therefore the babe assumes he or she has caused everything to happen. I must have thought I caused those losses; in the years to come I tried very hard to be good and any attempt to make me feel guilty was avoided with great vigor.

When my mother was released from the hospital, we moved back to Austin to be cared for by my grandmother and new directives were issued. Because they thought my mother might have had tuberculosis, I was told I shouldn't get too near her; certainly she shouldn't kiss me. All of this caused a rift in my feelings for her. I was never consciously aware of this, but I did know there was something that made me leery of her. I guess this was added to a sense of guilt over being my father's favorite. She was never anything but the most dedicated of mothers, but our relationship had a wound that lay beneath the surface of my awareness.

No story of my background would be complete without telling about Roy and Jenny. They were my imaginary playmates, and they accompanied me each day as I played and I left room for them wherever I might be. I remember realizing after I began school that they were no longer present and wondering where they were. Around that same time I noticed another strange change in my world. I had often played with Dorothy Gresham, the only other young girl who lived on Ruiz Street. We liked to "p'like"—an amalgamation of "play" and "like". One day we decided to plike we were our favorite movie stars as we had often done in the past. I walked out the lines on the ground that defined my ideal house, chose my favorite movie star, and tried to enter that imaginary world as usual. Then I found it was no longer there. I could no longer become Delores Del Rio and slide into that glamorous, tinsel make-believe world. What a loss!

My grandmother's house was in a significant location because it was close to the capitol building. That building was the hub of the town and to our family it seemed the most important spot on earth. It was so close that it seemed to loom over our back yard. Tall buildings blocked our view later on, but at that time my grandmother's kitchen window framed it for us, and, it seemed to be one more impressive picture in our art-filled home.

Ruiz Street was small and the surface was rounded to allow rainwater to drain into the gutters. So few cars traveled on Ruiz that it was safe to wade in the rainwater that collected in the gutters before draining off. The neighborhood yards were shaded with huge oaks and sidewalks bordered the road. During the torrid summer months the tar paving grew hot and soft under bare feet, and no hint foretold the fate of that little street that was to become the major artery of Lamar Boulevard when the town expanded into a busy city in years to come.

At the end of the block to the south, Ruiz intersected with 6th Street, where an amazing tower light stood. This was one of several in town that rose like powerful guardians of our safety to illuminate the area. Those lights were a source of pride in Austin, yet today their majestic existence seems to have been forgotten. I have been told that two are left standing but I'm sure their height is no longer impressive.

When I lived there as a small child, Ruiz Street was a melting pot. Among our neighbors were the Gannaways, Simpsons, the Doesterhofts, the Jacksons and the Lowensteins. I was the only small child on the street, and I often entertained myself by visiting these diverse families. They always welcomed me, and I was usually treated to cookies and a glass of milk as we held long conversations. I certainly didn't realize then how precious was this opportunity to experience those visits. Some of these were probably only second or third generation Americans, and that meant their homes still maintained a flavor of other cultures. Never was I treated as an unwelcome guest and I learned to value individual differences, although I didn't recognize it at the time. I never experienced fear of rejection when I approached those front doors and knocked to be let in, nor did I ever sense that I was an intruder.

Looking back, I only remember the feeling of those people and houses—their warmth, their orderliness; one was remembered because of its darkness, another for its strangeness. The Jackson's Christmas tree will always be remembered for its perfection. Tinfoil icicles hung from its branches, one after another each hanging exactly the same length as the next, carefully decorated by a compulsive family member.

The closest neighbor and the one I visited most often was Mrs. Gannaway, a widow who lived with her daughter, Miss Katie, and her architect son, Mr. Herbert Gannaway. I frequently visited Mrs. Gannaway, even as I grew older. She scrubbed their laundry in a huge tub under their house. Mr. Herbert no doubt designed and cleverly built it high off the ground leaving a dark, cool space beneath that served as a laundry room—a wonderful solution to escape the torrid heat of Austin summers. Wooden supporting beams hung low enough to invite my own artistic ventures, and I drew chalk illustrations meant to testify to the sudsing ability of her Rinso soap—small replicas of that hard working woman bent laboriously over a tub overflowing with suds.

* * *

I don't remember much about going to church, but after my mother's death I found amidst her keepsakes a certificate decorated with an accumulation of gold stars rewarded for my attendance at Sunday school. This calls to mind a favorite story from the family archive. When I was very young—probably three or four years old, I was asked to sing a solo in church. This was a big protestant church and the incident was quite an honor. I'm sure that my invitation evolved from my heritage—being an issue of the Pharr family of musicians. The family orchestra was popular and well known in Austin, and this must have endowed me with expectations. Surely a new star was to be born.

However, a misstep occurred when I did my thing; I was supposed to sing, "Jesus Loves the Little Children of the World", and I sang a perfect but errant rendition of "The Sidewalks of New York". My short-lived fame resulted from a boo-boo.

This evidently didn't bother me; as soon as I was old enough, I began singing in choirs. In those days Music was taught in schools and there was always a choir. Despite our frequent moves, I sang in school and church choirs and was always the star of the music classes. In one of the classes the teacher appointed me to direct the choir, a subterfuge that I imagine enabled her to disappear for the hour probably to smoke cigarettes in the teacher's lounge.

When I was eight years old, my aunt Charlotte became ill. By that time my father's work had caused us to move to another town each year. We were living away from Austin when Charlotte became sick, and mother took me out of school, and we returned to Austin for mother to take care of her. Charlotte's life dwindled away from September until she finally passed away on Christmas day. That beautiful angel who was loved by everyone who knew her and who loved me dearly was taken from us to leave a space in my heart that would never again be filled. Austin was never the same after she left.

A big change in my church attendance occurred when I was eleven years old. I had been going to a big protestant church along with most of my friends when a cousin came to visit us during a break in her college schedule. We felt it our duty to take her to her church that Sunday, and she was an Episcopalian. The minute I walked into the door of that church I was stunned. I was used to meeting in a building filled with people loudly conversing with one another before the service started. Complete quiet reigned in this church with people evidently sitting in contemplation.

Where I had previously attended, the choir sat facing the congregation, each person dressed in Sunday finery.

The Episcopal Church building was rather old and dark, and this helped create a feeling of reverence; it seemed to offer a haven from the world.

The first altar I'd ever seen stood ahead of me; it was covered with crisp white linen and one immediately sensed its importance. The flickering light from tall tapers held aloft on either side by ornate brass holders were reflected in the brass cross that stood in the center. This created a beauty beyond description then music began, and it was much more sophisticated than what I usually heard. I thought it was wonderful. The priest came in from the rear of the church led by an acolyte carrying a cross. My heart soared as the first truly spiritual feelings I had ever experienced flooded in to fill me with joy.

After attending it for a while, my mother, father and I all decided to join the church, and soon my father and I were baptized and the three of us were confirmed together. My music teacher from school was the choir director and I was immediately taken into the choir—the only child member. I was able to sing that glorious music. Choir members processed in behind the priest and sat in pews turned sideways to the congregation on either side of the sanctuary facing one another, and we were robed in white cottas that made us less conspicuous. I was in heaven. When the service ended, I would rush to doff my cotta and hurry to the front door to join the end the line of exiting members. This enabled me to shake Father Baughknight's soft warm hand as he peered at me with eyes that twinkled behind the coke bottle lenses of his glasses.

The Senior Altar Guild members knew a good thing when they saw it; I was quickly made a member of the Junior Altar Guild. Looking back on this, I don't remember any other members, but I do remember my first assignment. Somehow candles of wax had been put in the holders instead of the usual ones of tallow, and they began to melt during the service. I watched in horror as they bent in supplication during the service anointing the holders and the altar cloth with warm wax. The Junior Altar Guild was called to the rescue! I meticulously scraped the coating of melted wax off the holders feeling honored to be given that task; never were any candlestick holders cleaned with more reverence.

This transition between churches was not without discomfort. I left my many friends behind at the other church, and I don't remember knowing any other children at the church I had chosen. The Episcopalians were not noted for having the best youth program in this small town. But I was used to changes, and to being different, and I had found my home.

I have come to believe that how a person experiences God depends a lot on where, when, and with whom he or she enters and grows in this life. The essential thing is to recognize that something larger than our own self exists, and I believe we are born with this knowledge tucked away within our consciousness. We can ignore it, deny it, or call it by any name we choose, but its there. Recognizing there is a God means comfort and peace in a strife-filled world.

For me, I love the pageantry, the rituals, the beauty of my chosen church, but I sincerely believe that each person has the right to find their own way. I doubt that God cares whether you handle snakes or fast on Friday, but wants us to love and care for all of his creations. I do feel that recognizing you are not alone in this world gives you a feeling of peace no matter how difficult your life journey may be.

My father's work caused us to move every year during my school years. I went to fifteen schools in the twelve years of schooling that was required in those days. I adapted to this by learning to look forward to new environments, seeing the move as an opportunity to start fresh, and I didn't let myself spend time in grieving. My mother's tendency to become depressed over losses taught me that looking back and grieving was not fruitful and I didn't allow myself too much sorrow over leaving friends. I knew that change was inevitable and my challenge was to adapt to the new situation.

These were days when people didn't move about much, and a new girl always caused somewhat of a stir. I had also learned that my entry would be seen as a threat because it disturbed their settled world and the comfort of having things as they always were. I was an intruder for a while, and I learned to stay rather quiet and in the background until people in a new setting got used to me. Once they ceased to see me as a threat, I would slip into their social group. I became quite accomplished at this and never ended up lacking friends.

The fact that I was able to make all those moves with grace arose from my background. That little Ruiz Street visitor was used to differences. This prepared me to be able to work with the variety of individuals I encountered when I chose a career in the helping profession.

The problem that arises from such a loving environment is a naivety that sends one into a world that can be cruel at times. I was ill prepared to defend myself against an onslaught of less thoughtful, even mean, people and circumstances that would inevitably be encountered upon my life's journey.

Two unpleasant memories from early childhood occurred when I was away from home and was truly mistreated by adults in the environment. I remember feeling absolutely amazed at their attitude and had no idea what I had done that had offended them. The first hurtful incident occurred when I was very young and I was visiting my cousin. I had evidently monopolized her toys. My aunt called me a spoiled brat and indignantly took me home. I can only remember my surprise and lack of understanding of what I had done wrong. In my own defense I would say I was an only child with few toys and my cousin's family was well to do and had many; this must have been very tempting to an only child who hadn't learned sharing. I may have been a spoiled brat; I was unquestionably daddy's little princess.

The second incident happened when I was a little older. I was at a dance studio where I was taking lessons. I remember seeing the teacher through a glass window into her office. She was talking on the telephone to someone and suddenly slammed down the receiver and rushed out of her office; I was the first person she encountered. She inexplicably verbally attacked me! She was evidently very angry with someone and had displaced her anger onto me. I had no idea what was happening, but I remember my mother being present and allowing this to happen but not defending me. For some reason (doubtlessly it resulted from that scene), I didn't take any more dancing lessons and I was disappointed.

My mother was either unable to defend me because of her own internalized messages to be nice, or her inability to express her own anger. I do know that she always was afraid of any expression of annoyance. The result of her observing this mistreatment and not acting was a strong lesson for me that I had no right to defend myself, which meant it was one lesson that was left for my own learning.

I know my mother's family had always honored the Christian ethic of not striking back in anger or seeking vengeance. The thing that I needed to learn however was to be able to verbalize my own position without blame and to stand up for myself and not allow myself to be mistreated. Closely related to that is being able to ask for what you want or need. What not to learn is inappropriate self-sacrifice and passivity.

I have never led a flawless life; I made major mistakes if viewed from the stance of societal expectations. I wanted to be liked and to fit in, but at the same time I valued my individuality. Later, when I began studying Jung's view of personality development, I eagerly explored my inner spaces, particularly after I learned to meditate and work with dreams. I became dedicated to discovering the parts of me that I had unwittingly buried in an effort to please others or that I had not yet discovered. I sought wholeness. My ability to be assertive certainly needed to be discovered.

Each individual is born into a family and an environment that creates a matrix for their beingness. How one encounters and deals with the matters inherent within this matrix shapes his or her personal growth and maturity. This nest should provide nurturing and does present challenges to be faced as time passes. So it is that any individual's view of life evolves in a different way from anyone else's. My work at understanding myself trying to become more whole can hopefully help you conceptualize your own patterns of existence and better understand your own unfoldment. It is helpful to realize that the matrix of the family helps create the lessons you are meant to learn in this lifetime.

An abbreviated overview of my own little world reveals that I entered and was welcomed into my family of origin to become daddy's little princess. Only a few things happened along my way in early childhood that taught me that not all people are loving, but for the most part I learned that people were kind and that their differences were to be respected. My father was a gentle man and never treated women as subservient, but my mother's lack of self-confidence coupled with society dictates about a woman's role taught me that men had the power and thus were the source of security. I also viewed women's lives as dull, filled with repetitive tasks that were never finished and unrewarding. I did not recognize their strength, their power, or the value of their nurturing abilities until late in my life. I failed to recognize my own strengths for a long time, and I had to learn to take responsibility for myself as well as learn to stand up for myself. My genes contributed a love for music, art, and creative expression. I have always loved to discover the beauty in all things.

I know that there has tended to be a tug of war between the princess part of me that naively expects to be successful in all things and wants to sail ahead in pursuit of dreams while another part is cautious and fearful. This is apparent in what I say about the writing of this book. Part of me wants and need to tell my story; another part says, "Are you crazy? You'll reveal your faults and inadequacy and be seen as nut." This fearful part sabotages me at times.

However, there is good and bad, strength and weakness in all things. There are two sides to everything and often opposing views within your own mind cause conflict and "dys-ease". I have chosen to show you some ways to work with these inner disputes through the use of meditation and visualization and in order to resolve conflicts and utilize the positive aspects of each to reach a new level of understanding. For instance, my overzealous self-confidence can be tempered by the wisdom of that cautious part to enable me to more safely take off on new adventures. Without resolution of the conflict, I could be either be sabotaged by my naivety or the protector-self could take over and stultify my life.

The challenges we face in life seldom, if ever, get completely solved in one encounter. Personal growth occurs in a spiral-like series of skirmishes. If you are open to becoming more of who you were intended to be, each time you encounter that challenge it will be at a different level as you spiral upward. This transition often seems like a small death as we release old, limited ways of being and accept a new life. In fact, if you are committed to personal growth you will die and be reborn to a new way of being many times.

The journey is never smooth or flawless; we learn from the bumps and what seem to be detours along the way. I want to help you learn to draw upon your inner resources to enhance your life. Self-awareness is the first step on the journey to personal growth.

THE SECRET PLACE

When I was a small child,
I had a secret place
though no one ever knew
I claimed it.
It was a narrow space
between my grandmother's house
and the neighbor's fence,
behind the rain barrel
placed beneath the gutter spout
to capture rain
for washing hair.
Sun-starved,
the sandy earth there
was always cool,
even on the scorching
summer days,
and small, smooth pebbles
of pink and white
surprised my bare legs
with icy coldness
as I sat quietly
savoring the moments
stolen from play.
It was there that I
began to discover
what it was to be me.

Chapter 4
Individuation Process

Jung called the changes that occur as we grow older the individuation process. I'm sure your have recognized that the way you perceived the world and how you thought of yourself just a few years ago has evolved; it is different now from what it was then. This becomes even more apparent when you compare the very young person's sense of self to that of someone who is in the second half of life.

Joseph Campbell, Professor of Mythology, and TV journalist Bill Moyers presented a PBS series on mythology that was extremely popular. Moyers described Campbell as a remarkable man and legendary teacher. Campbell's classic advice to individuals was to "follow your bliss". He believed that success and happiness would follow if one made such a choice, and he was actually describing how to successfully go through the individuation process.

How we experience our own selfhood is an adaptation to life. It changes throughout life through the process of personal growth. When this occurs the experience is like a minor death-rebirth occasion. Individuals who are not very self-aware may not recognize this occurrence, but this is the way we grow and mature psychologically.

Our sense of identity changes drastically when we move into adulthood. We should leave behind our dependency on parents in order to create our own place in the world. As time goes on a man may marry and start his own family. A woman makes similar changes and life-altering decisions; she may marry and perhaps become a mother. If she works outside the home she also faces the challenge of combining work responsibilities with caring for husband and children. Each time we take a step that leads us in a new direction this is likely to change our adaptation in life (the way we see our self). The young woman who has said, "I am a student", or "I am a secretary", makes a change and instead says, "I am a wife", or "I am a mother". She is speaking about her sense of identity at that point in time.

How comfortable you feel about yourself results to a large degree in the many choices we are called upon to make. Do they reflect the person you truly are, or do you accommodate yourself to the expectations of others?

Have you chosen work that pays well but for which you have no natural bent? The choices artistic people must make provide an obvious example of difficult life choices they must face. An artistic person may not choose a career in that field because of the financial insecurity.

My own father grew up playing various musical instruments in the family orchestra but left music behind because playing in bands night after night and sleeping or practicing during the day didn't fit in well with family life. He changed from student and musician to husband and father in a short period of time because being a musician entailed uncertainty of regular work and the work hours did not jibe with family life.

A major change in my adaptation to life came when I divorced my children's father whom I had married when I was quite young. I knew that I needed a college education to support my children and myself. I fearfully took the entrance exams and I was able to enter the nearby Del Mar Jr. College. Later, I had to transfer to the University of Texas, another fearful experience.

I became aware that I had made that change successfully when I was driving to classes at the University one morning and my car passed one going in the opposite direction. A station wagon loaded with school-aged children all of whom were yelling loudly; the woman driving looked totally overwhelmed. A thought flashed through my mind: "Thank God that's not me." I looked at the notebook and texts next to me on the car seat and thought of the class that I would soon attend. I knew beyond a doubt that I was in the perfect place for me. At that moment I knew I had made it; I was really being "student-me", and that filled me with joy.

Change is always frightening because it requires a leap of faith. You never know what will happen or where it will lead. An insistent urging impels you to take that risk.

Sometimes that risk is simply too costly, especially when you are responsible for caring for other people. Pursuit of any of the Arts, for instance, means a period of financial instability because it always takes time to become established. Another problem is that the competitiveness involved with becoming well known in one's field doesn't fit easily with the artist's need for quiet time for creativity. Many times individuals put their natural talents on the back burner in order to make a living.

A few years ago I was talking with a doctor; when I mentioned that my late husband had been in the newspaper business and that I was an author, his eyes began sparkling with enthusiasm as he spoke about how much he liked to write and how he would have liked to have chosen that as a profession. Instead, he had made the "smart choice" and had obviously reaped the benefits of a thriving medical practice.

A few years later I saw him again briefly and I would not have recognized him as the same man. He had moved to more impressive offices, scads of patients impatiently sat in the waiting room. He rushed into the treatment room and instead of connecting with me in a personal way, in fact he did not even recognize me. He was playing catch-up because he had just returned from a vacation spent sailing in the Bahamas and was deeply tanned, but he did not look rested. He had made his choice and his life style was impressive, but no sparkle lit his eyes, no smile appeared on his face, and I could feel the burden of his huge practice. He choose a worthwhile and lucrative career over writing professionally, but he could still honor the part of himself that wants to write by giving it some space if it's only in keeping a journal.

Keeping a journal is a meaningful activity because it can serve as a link between the inner and outer reality and can connect the ego to the inner self. It also offers a rare opportunity for the writer to examine his or her life free of the scrutiny of others—to be real and that's meaningful.

Choosing a direction too far removed from our instincts may well hamper our unfoldment. Good mental health can be associated with recognizing and listening to one's inner voice. Don't sacrifice your gift; leave some time for the expression of those urgings even if only in a hobby.

I honored my artist self by painting quite a lot after being reminded of her existence in a visualization workshop.

I realized then how important it was to keeping painting even though I had chosen another career direction. I painted many a picture and many portraits even after I became a mental health professional and especially after I retired. Even when I write, (which is another form of artistry), I continue to paint.

Individuation simply means being your true self rather than thinking the façade you present to the world is the real you. This requires making decisions based on what is right for you rather than what is thrust upon you.

One of the problems that plague women is finding it difficult to say "no". They think their acceptance or popularity depends on pleasing others, and too often this causes them to do for others to the detriment of their own existence. Choose not to automatically do what others expect of you, or you give your individuality away.

Every choice we make presents an opportunity for growth. Every problem we face is an opportunity for growth. We find new ways of coping with life. Making conscious choices keeps us from falling into a passive mode.

When I am behaving in a passive way, I have often dreamed of being in a car but not driving. I may even be in the back seat. Sometimes I am driving up a mountain with a precipice on each side. Help! I may be driving a very heavy car that I have difficulty turning. Sometimes my car is skidding–going out of control. I've never had a dream wreck, thank goodness. The dream is simply saying to recognize your passivity, your lack of control, fear, or the risk you are taking. It may be saying that you are too burdened with responsibility and suggesting you ought to do something about it. If my car is skidding, I'm not handling things very efficiently; I'd better take control immediately.

When we find our self doing what is expected of us rather than what we really want to do, we are not being individualistic but are conforming. I had a dream that expresses the kind of conformity that is unhealthy for any person. It occurred when I had been working on a talk to be given to a rather large audience out of town. I wasn't satisfied with my explanation of individuation. The night before I left I had the following dream:

> Three women are performing a dance routine and singing. They are dressed in identical dresses and their hair is arranged perfectly alike. In one hand, each is holding a velvet covered rolling pin.

Who wants to conform to that extent? It reminds me of something I once read: "Shoulds" are someone else's rules.

Prior to this and after I had begun working with my dreams, I had my first "big dream" and it was about individuation. I called it "The Glass Giant" because of an expression used in that dream.

This dream message clearly pictures my journey in life. It's as if the dream says, "At this point in time you need to enrich your life by getting in touch with and bringing forth the masculine principle that resides within—your more assertive part. You need to uncover your potential and become a more effective person."

When the dream-maker knows you are interested in and take dreams seriously, it seems to work overtime to give you plenty of material. A particularly important dream has a numinous quality about the experience—an energy charge that causes you to remember the dream with a certainty about its importance. This energy actually inflates the ego. When you experience this, you are ready to go out and preach to the world, and it's easy to think you are an authority on the subject. So it was that the Giant dream was so impressive that I was inspired to write about it. As time passed, the energy dissipated and the impulse diminished, but by the time my inflation from this dream lessened to a realistic size, I had outlined several chapters and started writing. In one way, it was the origin of this present book that is being written much later in life.

"The Glass Giant" was a significant dream because it described the growth process of the psyche. It resulted from my conscious effort to grow and my accepting attitude toward whatever the dream-maker would produce. It showed me what was in store for me in the future—the way my personality needed to unfold so that I could become more of the person I was meant to be. The Glass Giant dream follows:

Scene 1. I am in a large arena; no walls are visible, but I have the feeling that the area was round and that there is some kind of a very high domed ceiling. People are moving about, and I am a member of this group although I am not interacting with anyone. I have a sheltered feeling.

Scene 2. I have worked out in a gym, have showered and dressed in clean clothes. I approach a central staircase leading downward. Moving against the flow of traffic, I descend to a lower level where people are dining, but I have already eaten, and walk past them seeking a rest room.

Scene 3. I go to the restroom, and then retrace my steps to ascend the stairs. At the top a large man seems to await me. His appearance is sort of rumpled; his dark blue suit is wrinkled and his smile reveals cream yellow teeth. I notice a few pieces of straw or hay as if he may have been asleep in a haystack. He isn't particularly handsome, but he has a nice smile and I feel his warmth, strength and his appreciation of me.

He looks down at me, smiles and says, "You are just the kind of woman I like—a glass giant." Then, he brushes past me and goes his way, but I know we will meet again and I am pleased.

When I awoke, I was excited and anxious to think about the phrase "glass giant" What on earth did it mean? At least it seemed positive.

Jung spoke of the shadow as the part of our self that lies outside our awareness. We only see our facade–the face we show to the world. When a woman dreams of a man, he symbolizes the shadow; he is called her animus. Likewise when a man dreams of a woman she would be his feminine aspect–his anima. I was looking out at the world through eyes typical of that point in time–I saw men as the ones in charge, the decision-makers by right. Even after a divorce and being out on my own, I felt I was doing "the forbidden thing" in more ways that one; I was supposed to be at home raising children. I really didn't have clarity about how I could "be" in this world. The man at the top of the stairs was an aspect of self that had not fully come forth at this time.

The round, dome-like place which was the setting of this dream is "my world" and being circular would stand for wholeness. Since I had been downstairs and had gone to the rest room I would have worked through something that needed to be tended to in order for me to move up to the next level of consciousness, so to speak.

That much was easy to understand, but what did the "glass giant" mean? I meditated on it and I saw the glass lamp that sat on an end table next to the divan in my office; I saw it every day as I worked. The glass was solid and very heavy, and a series of curves rose to the light. Inside that glass was a silver rod that held the cord and it was plugged into the electrical outlet. A pleated shade hid the light bulb and reflected the light outward to illuminate the room.

There was nothing fragile about that lamp; it would have taken a major disaster to break it. Its curves spoke of femininity and that silver rod symbolized the center of self. All of this was reassuring because the word "giant" could easily have meant inflation of the ego; I chose to think of it as the inflation that occurs naturally from the energy involved in a break through of information from the unconscious mind. I decided the glass was a symbol for my intuitive understanding instead of meaning fragility; the lamp was too sturdy for that to ring true.

The important thing about the lamp was that it provided the light of understanding and that light issued forth through its connection to the source of energy, God's way of constantly creating the world in which we live. If we are receptive to the energy of Spirit we will move toward being who we were created to be.

Just like that acorn is destined to become an oak tree, so do we have an inner potential. That oak needs space in which to grow and rain and sun to nourish it; self-awareness is our way of helping ourselves become more of who we are meant to be.

WOMAN

Woman—
complementing,
molding self
around edges
and protrusions,
defined by
what she is not.
Woman- -pulls away,
finds no matrix
for restructuring,
waits expectantly
to be pushed back
by space,
and for a time,
longs for the absent boundaries—
something to lean against—
to be imprisoned by?
Reminds herself
that boundaries
can be restraining walls.
Now she is beginning
to define space by her presence
and reaches out
for what she wants.
She forms old words
with new found pleasure.
"I am woman."

TO MAN

You shoot straight arrows
at distant targets
while I sort through
kaleidoscopic days
and know a rounder,
more chaotic Truth
than you perceive.
Each of us is powerful
although my strength
may be more difficult to see,
and it's tempting
not to value
such ephemeral ways.
If you fail to recognize my worth
we'll both have lost life's promise.
If you see me as a threat
and use your power to subdue me,
you'll suffer my anger,
though it may be indirect.
It's important to remember
each of us is vulnerable to pain.
Each was created
to complement each other,
meant to come together—
my softly yielding flesh welcoming
your hard body.
Man, will you honor my gentleness,
recognize my strength and
receive the tenderness,
of my nurturing?
I was meant to be with you.

Chapter 5
The Mind-body Connection

The connection between mind and body is very real, but no description can accurately portray its true nature. Working as a counselor, I became aware of how often a client's physical discomfort reflected the stress that person was experiencing in life.

For instance, an overworked volunteer secretary of a small church came in for counseling because her hand and arm were hurting so badly that it was becoming impossible for her to perform the task of keeping the books. She was one of a group of individuals who founded the church, and she had volunteered to do the job without pay as her contribution to its existence. However, one member was constantly causing trouble. If my client resigned, it would mean giving up her means of supporting the church's continuation. Moreover, this particular church stressed positive thinking. To quit because of her dislike of the troublemaker made her feel she was not living up to her beliefs.

The first thing to do was address her own pain so that the part of herself who felt mistreated would know it was heard and understood. Feelings like anger and an urge to seek revenge are real. It doesn't work to tell yourself you shouldn't feel that way. What you do in response to them is something else. I heard an expression once that I like to repeat under these circumstances: "You aren't responsible for the birds that fly over your head, but you are if you let them nest in it."

The next step was to devise ways the client might confront the complainer in a non-blaming manner to avoid an argument that could result in blaming and bitterness. "I statements" are the best way to do this. "I feel–" instead of "You make me–" doesn't arouse the other person's defense mechanisms. Our goal was to establish a climate where differences could be worked out. The complainer needed to be heard. Sometimes, complaints occur when a person wants to be seen as important and needed. Perhaps his energy could be re-directed in a helpful manner.

Our efforts worked out, and the client's physical problems cleared up afterwards. She also learned that physical symptoms may occur in the future anytime she isn't dealing with a problem.

Back pain often happens when an individual is carrying a lot of responsibility in life. If you think of other phrases that refer to body parts, it's easy to see why that analogy came about. Phrases like, "you're a pain in the neck, I can't stomach it, that job is a headache, you make me sick at my stomach" have become trite because they are so descriptive of where stress manifests in the body.

Pain is unpleasant and we would like to avoid it, but it is a symptom and serves a purpose; it tells us something we are doing is dysfunctional. If your hand touches fire, you pull it away from the flame. Recognize the cause of the discomfort, and you can make a change for the better.

I observed my own asthma and realized that it can serve as a red flag to warn me that I may be allergic to something in the environment, or it can also be caused by stress. My chest tightens up when I feel endangered or pressured. Long periods of time may pass by without any attacks, but when I am experiencing something unusually stressful, or I am overly tired, I am likely to have breathing problems. It is a signal that I should deal with the cause, whether it is an allergy or stress.

Excellent medication is now available to ward off or treat attacks. If you have asthma, you know that when you lie down, it becomes harder to breathe because your bronchial passages will begin to tighten up. When you are asleep and begin having asthma, it is distressing. When it occurs to me, I am likely to awaken with an anxiety dream. Now that I am older, the dream may be that I am running away from some danger. When I was younger and working, the dream would likely be that I was trying to fly and not being able to get off the ground. If I did manage to take off, I would not be able to rise high enough, or power lines might endanger me.

One of these occasions brought on a dream that told me exactly what caused the attack, and I was able to work with it with amazing results. I was experiencing a lot of stress during that period of my life, and I began having asthma after being free of it for a few years.

I left Family Service Center after working there about five years to enter private practice. Every potential client who called for an appointment was important; I scrambled to see clients at their convenience. I worked earlier and stayed late if that was needed. To complicate matters, members of my profession were at that time seeking State licensing in order to define minimum qualifications for people who worked as counselors. This meant traveling to Austin to urge legislators to support our bill and sit conspicuously in the gallery to demonstrate our determination to get our bill passed.

All of this was taking its toll on my stamina. I awoke with asthma in the middle of the night, and in the midst of a dream.

> Scene 1. I see a room so full of things that I can't enter it. I walk around to the opposite side of the room and find a door that gives me access.

I woke up short of breath, and because I had been working with visualization a lot at that time, I immediately asked for a symbol for the cause of the asthma. I was half-asleep, but I planned to dialogue with the symbol to access information from my unconscious mind about its origin. No dialogue was needed; the answer immediately unfolded like a vision:

> Scene 2. I see a seated Buddha-like figure. The corners of square napkins are tied to one another to form cloth ropes that extend out from her in several directions.

I am stunned by the figure. It didn't appear to be human and I realized it must be an archetypal pattern of a counselor. She had ties to people and things for which she felt responsible. I noted with amusement that the ties were man-made ropes of soft cloth–nothing so crass as strings. These were like some napkins tied to make a trim for curtains that I had seen the pervious day in a restaurant.

The moment I saw her I knew that my counselor role had taken over and was running my life. The tail was wagging the dog! I also knew that all I had to do was take control and cut back on what I was doing.

An amazing thing happened at that moment. My asthma disappeared. It didn't leave slowly, or gradually, like it would have from the proper medication; it simply disappeared. It left from one breath to another!

Here I was in the middle of the night–elated. I wanted to shout, "My asthma is gone!" It was difficult to calm down enough to go back to sleep, but I finally made it.

I awoke jubilantly the next morning; I knew what to do to simplify my life. It was so simple–all I had to do was take control. This would involve taking a critical look at my schedule and canceling a few appointments. That was the answer to the immediate situation, but it was only after a period of time, that I realized the depth of the problem or the solution. I had not been in control of my life in the truest sense of the word. How fascinating that my unconscious mind held the information I needed and I had been able to access it.

I hadn't been adrift in a rudderless boat. I had set goals and reached them. I had extricated myself from a bad marriage, had gotten an education, gone to work at Family Service Center, and entered private practice. I obviously had made a lot of decisions, and good one, but they were made based on matters that pertained to security and to the general direction I wanted to take in life. I was tending to business, but I had neglected paying attention to the daily choices that were affecting my health.

That message from my childhood was dictating what I was "supposed to do". I may have entered the business world, but I was still operating out of the old pattern where a woman's role in life was one of serving others.

The result of this kind of stance is that you can easily end up doing things you don't really want to do and not enough time or energy is left for what you really want. You can end up feeling manipulated, used, or unappreciated by others. I had not considered my own individuality. I recognized and was responsible for meeting my physical needs, but I had never consciously expanded that to include my own preferences and desires. It was a long time before I realized I had a choice in the matter.

Not making a choice was opting to give someone else control over decision-making. When I didn't choose, I was forfeiting my right to at least ask for what I wanted or needed. Because I was familiar with the discomfort of being manipulated, I never wanted to do that to another person. I hadn't realized that making choices does not necessarily mean dominating others or always having to be the leader. It means choosing not to take a self-sacrificing role. I speak of the "power to do" rather than "power over". It is the difference between being offensively aggressive and assertive.

Thinking in terms of my asthma, I knew that when I pushed myself too hard I was likely to have asthma, yet I ignored my own physical need and I paid a price for it.

In those days people didn't think in terms of prevention, or of being responsible for the care of their body. They thought illness was something that unfortunately happened to them. They went to the doctor when they were sick and got medication to treat symptoms. There is a hidden payoff that accompanies illness; you have the perfect excuse not to perform your duties. Being sick throws you into a state of dependency, especially if it is bad enough to send you to the hospital. It gives you a chance to legitimately let others take care of you and thus get your dependency needs met.

Some of us, however, woke up along the way; a paradigm shift was about to take place. We were beginning to realize that taking care of the body would promote good health. We were beginning to recognize the undeniable (yet invisible) connection between body and mind, and we were recognizing how inner feelings could cause the body to suffer and even sicken. Most importantly, it caused us to take seriously the concept of being responsible for our life.

Instead of saying "that person" or "that thing makes me sick", we began to recognize our own role in the victimization. Instead of projecting blame onto others, we had to look at our role in the game we were inadvertently playing. When bad things happen, one needs to make changes. We can only change the way we are handling our own lives; we can't change another person. However, when we change, that other person must respond to us in a different way.

Those were the days when women were beginning to ask, "Who am I?" The culture had defined us as appendages to men; we were meant to have babies, cook, and tend to houses and husbands. We regarded that as the natural way to do things, and this was reinforced by the fact that men were our source of financial security. That began to change during the Second World War when Rosie discovered she liked to rivet.

I had learned to play that traditional, subservient role, but after 18 years of a troubled marriage and two children,

I found myself frequently complaining to my friends about my life. I was playing a great game of "poor me". Then one day I accidentally overheard a conversation between two women; one was the wife of a doctor. She said, "My husband says we get what we want out of life. If a person is unhappy, it means that's the way they want it."

I was shocked. I didn't agree with the statement; it hit too close to home. I had to face the fact that I wanted to be financially secure more than I wanted to face the many problems that would face me as a wage earner with children to raise alone. I didn't like to accept that, but it did make me evaluate my situation. I realized I should either do something about my situation or get out. I had no inkling about what to do to change the marriage, therefore, I decided to file for divorce. It wasn't easy. My decision tore my life asunder, but that needed to happen. One must sometimes clear out the old to make room for rebuilding.

Divorce was not the common occurrence it is today. I felt like someone outside of "normal society", but I was free at last–really free for the first time in my life. My first important choice was to go to college. I had married when I was very young–just out of high school and I wanted to be able to make a decent living for my children and myself and that meant I needed to get an education.

During the marriage, I had suffered a lot with asthma. I took a lot of medication and got allergy shots, however, a day came when I was sick and nothing seemed to be helping me get well. I stayed in bed and waited to recover, but that didn't work. The doctor was worried about my condition; he said it could become chronic, intractable asthma. That shocked me to the core, and I realized that being an invalid was absolutely unacceptable. Looking back, I realize that I made a conscious choice at that point to change my life.

Once I had recovered, I filed suit for divorce. This was frightening because I wasn't sure that my health would allow me to make a living and take care of my children. The process drug on painfully–a year passed before I got into court and the divorce was granted. Then, I was thrust into the single world with no handy manual to instruct me on survival. However, through the divorce settlement I was able to further my education and eventually become a mental health professional.

My health had drastically improved once I was out of the marriage. I never missed a day of classes in undergraduate or graduate school because of illness. The asthma didn't return until several years later when I allowed myself to become tired and stressed by my work and political activity. The experience of ridding myself of the asthma attack meant that I had recognized the potential efficacy of working with symbolic visualization. This was exciting. Surely it would be an invaluable tool for working with emotional illnesses. It did prove very helpful in many ways, but it has remained an illusive tool–never a sure thing.

A short time after I had the experience of having had my asthma instantly cease through visualization, I got a chance to attend a workshop for exploring the connection between body and mind and using symbolic imagery in the treatment of medical conditions.

Stephanie Symington, a mental health professional, and her husband, Dr. Carl Symington, were breaking new ground in the treatment of cancer patients. They used a team approach. Medical personnel administered treatment for the cancer. Mrs. Symington's role was to empower patients to fight their illness through visualization using symbols.

The first step in her therapy was to help patients discover how they viewed their cancer. The word "cancer" was enough to strike fear in any patient; the stigma of it was almost overpowering. The goal was to change their outlook, when possible, from fear and helplessness to one of strength and to give them hope.

She had the patient draw a picture of how they saw their cancer. The therapist would then explain that cancer cells were weak and confused which made them vulnerable to a strong opponent.

Many patients would commonly draw their cancer with a mass of vivid colors using irregular, jagged lines. Then she would have them draw something powerful, like an army, or a knight in shining armor, to arrive and attack the cancer symbol and eradicate it.

The approach was successful some of the time, but couldn't be relied upon with certainty. Sometimes, the problem lay outside the awareness of the patient or the doctor. For instance, the patient might have unconsciously decided to die. Even the lack of interest in living would rob the patient of the energy or motivation to fight.

A good example of this attitude occurred in that very workshop. One cancer patient, a woman with breast cancer, and her husband attended the first session although the workshop was designed for mental health professionals. The dynamics were fascinating. The husband pushed and pushed his wife to at least believe in the possibility of overcoming the illness. He tried desperately to get her to marshal her energy and fight, but it was obvious that she had no desire or intention to do it.

After the couple left, the observing therapists expressed the belief that her passivity probably reflected years of being dominated, and she had given up her desire to live. This was probably accurate, but before you blame the husband, ask yourself to examine her role. She may have allowed the domination, even welcomed it, as a method of avoiding responsibility and remaining in a childlike adaptation to life. Effective early therapeutic intervention might well have prevented this from happening.

The workshop was very informative, and provided me with an opportunity to share my story of ending my asthma attack. I told the story to a psychologist who was Mrs. Symington's assistant, and he gave me some feedback. He said that my dramatic success probably came from having been so close to the sleep state when the unconscious was more easily accessible.

Even though he pointed out the unusual circumstances of my experience, I returned to work energized and enthusiastic about using visualization when appropriate. I had one outstanding success when a client of mine had a tumor on her ovary. She was a nurse and a doctor's wife, so it was easy for her to visualize her condition. I suggested she visualize the tumor going away, and sure enough, when she was checking in for the surgery, X rays revealed that the tumor was no longer there. The experience impressed her so much that she later became a psychiatric nurse.

I became aware of another facet of the mind/body connection when a young woman came to me for help. She had grown up in Houston, but was living elsewhere. She was living in a very frustrating situation, and a friend happened to be a former client of mine and encouraged her to come to me.

Jane (the name adopted for telling her story) had problems that had evolved from having been adopted. Her adoptive parents believed that they were unable to have children, and adopted her, but a couple of years later, the woman became pregnant and gave birth to twin girls.

The father died unexpectedly a year or so later, leaving his wife to take care of the three small children. The stress caused her to turn to alcohol as an escape. Although Jane, herself, was still a child, she became the caretaker of an alcoholic and had to play substitute mother for the twin girls. Then, the alcoholic mother died, and Jane became totally responsible for the twins.

Jane had been told that she was adopted, and this was apparent since she was the only brunette in a family of blondes. The differences were more than in appearance, however. She realized that she was stronger than the women in her adoptive family. Her interests were very different, too. She loved music and began singing professionally while still in her teens, which spawned a belief that her blood relatives were possibly musicians.

Jane was a fascinating young woman; her face was beautiful, but her body had a rather shapeless, matronly look, and this impression proved to have some validity. In recounting her story, she mentioned that a doctor she had seen had remarked that her body was similar to a forty-year-old woman's.

The presenting problem for which she sought counseling, was that in her adoptive mother's will, instructions had been left that Jane was to be given her natural mother's name when she was twenty-one years old. This information was now in her hands, and Jane wanted to look for her, but this decision was fraught with danger. What if her mother did not want to acknowledge the birth?

Jane would feel this as a second rejection, and that could be devastating. However, with my encouragement, she began her search.

I did not hear from her for a short while, then, a jubilant Jane called. She had been reunited with her natural mother who lived in California. Her mother and her husband had been traveling in a motor home and had car trouble outside of Houston. While waiting for their vehicle to be repaired, her mother had somehow obtained information that eventually enabled her to contact Jane and had provided plane tickets for Jane to visit.

She told me the story of this adventure when she returned. Jane had walked down the stairs exiting the plane while fearfully wondering how she would know her mother. Instantly, she focused on a woman who stood, eagerly awaiting her arrival. Without hesitation, they flew into each other's arms.

Her mother told her the story of her birth and adoption. The pregnancy had occurred when she was very young and marrying the father was not an option. She was unable to care for the baby and had regretfully put her up for adoption. All of her life, she had openly acknowledged Jane's existence and had told her husband about the birth before their marriage. When children arrived, they were also told of Jane's existence, and it had always been understood that some day she would take her place in the family if she could be found. Jane's newfound stepsisters and stepfather welcomed her with love, as did her extended family.

Both of Jane's mother and natural father were of Italian descent, and her father was a musician. The love of music was deeply ingrained in the family members, and the women were strong, just as Jane had believed them to be.

Both Jane and I felt we had experienced a miracle, even to the interrupted trip that provided the opportunity for her mother to get information that lead her to finding Jane.

Jane made it possible for her twin adoptive sisters to see me for counseling to help them adjust to the changes caused by Jane's altered role and to encourage them to take responsibility in their lives. This also helped Jane avoid possible guilt feelings as she pulled away to join her natural family.

I believe that Jane's body reflected the fact that she had been forced to mature ahead of time as she assumed the role of mother. I have often wondered if her body changed after she was freed from that responsibility. I don't know. One of the tasks of a therapist is to let go of the client when the time comes so that he or she may leave counseling free of dependency ties, and I did not see her again.

Sometimes dreams will tell you about some physical problem before you recognize it. A psychiatrist I knew had a patient who dreamed of a foreign object in a house prior to doctors discovering he had a brain tumor. A pregnant friend of mine dreamt that enemies of some kind were parachuting into an airplane hanger to cause trouble. She soon learned that she had Rh-negative blood, and the condition threatened the life of her baby. Blood transfusions at birth saved the baby's life.

That inner voice may be heard in a dream, in intuition, or during meditation. Always check it out. It may well be Spirit sending you a message.

PATTERNS OF PERCEPTION

Memories
etched in one's mind
form patterns of perception
that paint
an endless tomorrow's
worth of days unquestioned.
What is real
is not irrevocably cast
in matter,
but shifts like
changing cloud forms
in a universal sky.

Chapter 6
Meditation And Visualization

I learned to meditate in the late sixties, when it was something new to this culture. At that time, a lot of people thought the practice was tied to eastern religious beliefs and regarded it with suspicion.

Perhaps they feared they would come out of their inward journey believing in a different religion. That fear could be seen as a lack of faith. Others expressed fear of losing control, but loss control of what?

Meditation can be used as a silent prayer. It is now often also used in this culture as a relaxation technique–a method of lowering blood pressure and counteracting other symptoms of stress.

Meditation used in worship allows spiritual feelings to emerge. In meditation, one does feel a connection with all of creation, and that encourages good stewardship of the planet and concern for the wellbeing of others. One of the most valuable results of meditating on a regular basis is the feeling of being centered that accompanies your return to the outer reality, enhancing your ability to function in this complicated world with patience and efficiency.

The act of meditation is to turn inward with a relaxed, but with focused concentration. You should first find a quiet spot where you are not likely to be interrupted. It is helpful to return to that same place each time you meditate; it will become associated with that practice and help you to achieve the meditative state.

Having pets around you is not encouraged because they may find your silence very interesting and bother you. However, I have both a dog and a cat and they simply ignore me.

You should loosen any clothing that binds you or it might interfere with your comfort or circulation. Sit in a chair with your feet comfortably on the floor and your hands resting in your lap—no crossed limbs. If you are sitting in an uncomfortable position you'll never get there.

There are many ways to meditate, and the suggestions given here are a simplified overview. To meditate, one first has to turn inward and quiet the mind. One way to take your attention off of the environment is by focusing on a mantra. I learned by taking a class in Transcendental Meditation, and each student is assigned a mantra. However, "aum" is a universal mantra, pronounced ah-um (two syllables) and can be used by anyone. If you use a mantra, you are encouraged not to say it out loud or tell anyone else what it is. This makes it associated with the practice and helps you get into the meditative state rapidly. Observing your breathing is another way to focus. Some people observe a candle's flame then remember the candle's flame when they close your eyes or when it goes out.

If you have any misgivings about going into the meditative state of consciousness, start with a prayer and declare that you are guarded from any harm by your faith in Jesus Christ. If you are not a Christian, you may choose any other way you wish to express you belief in a protective Higher Power.

Close your eyes and focus inward; begin silently repeating your mantra, if you are using one, silently and in a relaxed way. When you are in an ordinary state of consciousness and interacting with the environment, your brain produces beta waves. In meditation they slow down from beta and dip into alpha. Thoughts will emerge at times; you can be saying your mantra and suddenly find yourself thinking of some mundane thing such as what you need from the grocery store. A common reaction is to use mental effort to get your brain to "behave". However, it isn't misbehaving; it's doing its natural thing. Trying harder is the opposite of what is needed. Instead, calmly return to silently repeating your mantra or whatever tool you are using for concentration.

Any noise, especially a telephone that rings, is startling and causes an unpleasant jangled feeling. If this happens, you need to return to the meditative state to regain your relaxed feeling as soon as possible. Don't just give up and quit because you will find yourself left in a disgruntled mood. A successful meditation leaves you feeling wonderfully relaxed and in good humor.

The suggested time for meditation is fifteen to twenty minutes. If you merely stay quiet for that length of time, you will feel relaxed. When you first start meditating, you may question whether you have actually done it. People tend to expect weird things to happen; some expect to go into a trance, others think they should be able to stop thinking about anything at all. These mistaken expectations cause disappointment and a feeling of failure that may cause the person to quit trying. Don't set yourself up for failure by unrealistic expectations. When you come out of meditation, do so slowly to retain your sense of peacefulness. The distinctive rewards of meditating come as you practice it over a period of time.

Meditation can purposely be used as a problem solving technique. If you want the answer to a question, just take it into meditation with you. Let go, and the clearest answers imaginable will pop into your mind. In other words, don't try to use your ordinary way of solving a problem–just ask for an answer and get out of the way. The answer will pop into your mind, and it will not be tainted by your ego's desire to further its own importance. The answer will be wisdom in the purest sense.

Many books have been written on Christian contemplation. This involves taking a reading from the Bible into the silence and letting it speak to you, which is very valuable. To me, prayer given as a laundry list of requests is not as meaningful as simply becoming silent and becoming aware of the presence of Spirit and being receptive to what you hear with the ear of the heart.

To me, the deepest and most fruitful form of meditation results from concentration on a mantra. This requires learning to get past the "chitch" (the errant thoughts that keep intruding).

* * *

Visualization is a tool used for personal growth and to discern the meaning of symbols and metaphors. It gives the imagination reign and encourages material to arise from beyond the threshold of our ordinary consciousness. There are as many ways to use it as the imagination can produce, and you may hear it called by other names, such as active imagination or imagery.

It can be done in two basic ways: imagery done alone and guided imagery, which is used in therapy sessions and in other types of groups. The latter requires one person to serve as a guide. He or she directs others through a predetermined exercise or, (as with therapy), asks questions that allow answers with helpful information to surface. The persons who follow instructions are asked to close their eyes and let their imagination take over. It helps if they know how to meditate because they need to be comfortable and have the ability and willingness to let go of control.

If these suggestions arouse fear in anyone, that person may simply decide not to take part. Anyone who happens to become frightened during the imagery can simply open their eyes, and they will immediately return to their usual state of consciousness.

The following example is of a guided visualization, and the kind of message that it can reveal. I was attending a workshop on guided imagery given in Houston after I had been meditating for around a year. The workshop was not given in a religious setting but offered an opportunity to learn to use meditation to increase self-awareness. In those days this was a cutting-edge thing to do. The presenter was Joannne Cusak, a popular psychic who had an office in Houston and traveled to outlying towns giving readings.

During that workshop and after doing some exercises that utilized the meditative state of consciousness, she said, "There is a source of wisdom within you that you can consult when you want to understand something more deeply or want help in making a decision. Ask your inner guide to come forth so that you can meet this wise old person who exists within you. It may be either a man or a woman".

To my amazement I saw quite clearly an old man come in as if he had been off stage to my right. He had a white beard and was dressed in a long white robe with a thick white cord tied around his waist that hung down ending with a knot and tassel.

Then Joanne said, "Ask him for some signal you can use to call him forth when you want to seek his wisdom." I saw the white rope-like cord that had been tied around his robe. I knew I was to pull it when I wanted to call him.

At some point we were asked to see a dot of color that would also indicate his presence. Some people see a lot of color when they close their eyes, but I usually see only darkness. When she asked for that dot of light, I saw a brilliant little spot of bluish-purple light and that same color comes to me in meditation and when I am waiting for sleep. When I see it I know that sleep is on its way, and the dot spreads out fluidly to cover the darkness as I drift into sleep.

Joanne did not assign any spiritual meaning to this use of meditation, but I came to believe that inner source of wisdom is Higher Self—the part of us that is the Christ Within.

I can understand that a church would feel it is not its role to teach such techniques or to encourage discovering an inner guide, although many New Age churches do stress the importance of meditation. The danger lies in the fact that many people would credit their own ego with being the source of this profound wisdom. This is an invitation to hubris (the excessive pride that could lead to the downfall of anyone who tried to steal the power of the gods, such as in mythical tragedies). In Greek mythology Daedalus made wax wings for his son, Icarus, but warned him to fly too close to the sun or they would melt. Icarus did not heed his father's warning, the wings melted, and he plunged into the sea and drowned.

The point of meditation is to align your consciousness in such a way that you invite Spirit to speak to and through you. To use what you are given in a self-deceptive way or a way that is exploitive to others is where the danger lies. Creative individuals would be wise to always give thanks to God for their talent and for anything they have created. Thinking your ego is the creator invites problems.

A wonderful example of the wisdom that can emerge from meditation happened to me when I was attending a weekly Jungian class taught by Veniece Standley in Houston. She explained that she wanted us to recognize the message given us by our well-meaning parents as opposed to the God-given message meant for us when we were created. She instructed us to sit in a comfortable position and close our eyes. When we were quiet and relaxed, she led in the following exercise:

"Imagine that you are walking through a forest. Tall trees surround you as you walk along a path that leads into the very center of the forest. The path is smooth beneath your feet. Sunlight filters through tree branches to form slender streaks of light. The air is cool and laden with the scent of the trees. A feeling of peacefulness permeates your being.

"Ahead of you in the path is a large rock. A message for you is engraved across it. Walk up to the rock and read what is written there. Your parents and those who were near and dear to you delivered this message when you were very small. The message instructs you how you should be in this world. " (The guide allows time for this to happen.)

"Walk farther down the path. There is another rock, and it also has a message written on it. This message is from a Higher Source. It is the Truth that tells you who you were created to be."

As soon as the leader asked us to see the message on the first rock, I saw the word, "Perform", emblazoned on it in letters that almost glowed with brilliance. The second rock instantly presented a message etched with equal splendor and containing astounding wisdom: "Blossom", it said.

It was clear to me that parents teach us how to get along in this world, but our personality, (who we are) is meant to unfold as we mature instead of being structured by the expectations of others, no matter how well intentioned they may be.

In this meditation we were instructed to take the revealed message from Higher Self of how we were intended to be and place it somewhere within our body or mind so that it would always be available to us. When we had made sure that the message was internalized, we could retrace our steps. When we returned to the place where we began our journey, we were to slowly open our eyes and return to the outer reality.

This was an exercise in guided imagery that shows how one can call for and receive information from the unconscious that can be used for personal growth. The feeling that flooded me at receiving those messages was joy and relief. I had discovered a basic truth that formed the very essence of my being. To blossom was to be given permission to be the person I was meant to be, and any blossom created by God is by nature beautiful.

When thinking about it later, I realized how that message would ring true for anyone. Parents want that wonderful little babe, who has been entrusted into their care, to grow into a worthwhile human being. Parents try their best to give their offspring every bit of instruction, every piece of information, needed to survive and flourish in this world. In the end, however, some of those messages can work to diminish our experience of life and must be recognized, examined, and altered or released. This is not an easy task, but an essential one for growth.

Imagery done with clients can help them discover the root-cause of the discomfort that caused them to seek counseling. However the "presenting problem" lies on the surface of their awareness, but they haven't been able to access the unconscious material where the root of the problem lies buried. For this reason they haven't been able to work through it and have tried ineffectively to brush it off, or get rid of it. Most people do not seek help readily because they see this as a sign of weakness. Nothing could be further from the truth; getting help is practical since they may need help to reach it. Once you have been taught some tools like meditation and visualization you can more easily do the weeding in the garden of your thought processes that allows you to function in a fruitful way.

Let me once again offer one of my own hang-ups to use as an example. You have been told about the age in which I lived and the societal circumstances that helped create my "daddy's little princess" syndrome. Very similar and undoubtedly related to that is my "Miss Goody-two-shoes". Understand that this was the way I earned my cookies; it served me well.

Lets skip ahead to adulthood at a time when I discovered something about myself one day. I was shopping in a department store and noticed that I was standing at a counter looking at a display of jewelry with my hands behind my back. This happened at a time when I was using imagery with clients, so I decided to make my own little journey to the land of the hidden past. I went after it in meditation and discovered an interesting little story.

I grew up during the depression and my family suffered along with others, at least to some extent. One of the ways of coping was to convert the dining room into a gift shop offering my artistic mother and grandmother's arts and crafts for sale. The most impressive project was one of my mother's. She received a commission to create the clothes for an entire wedding party of dolls as a Christmas present for the Austin City Manager's daughter. Every little item, such as lace trimmed underwear and tiny shoes crocheted out of gold thread, she designed and sewed to perfection. What an achievement!

Other items she sold were small ceramic bowls that she ordered from a catalogue and decorated with painted designs. However, my favorite items were small chiffon and lace trimmed decorative handkerchiefs with pictures painted on one corner of a pretty girl. These were entirely her own creation and entailed extremely intricate work, and anything she created was perfection itself.

How anyone even knew the little shop existed, I don't know. I do remember how fascinated I was at the process of her painting. I was allowed to stand and watch, but only if I were quiet, still, and kept my hands clasped behind my back. To touch the paint would be the greatest of sins. I had to wait until I was given a set of oil paints on my twelfth birthday to get my hands on those paints.

Good girls in those days were raised not to be a pest and bother people with questions or grab for things they shouldn't touch. It could also be considered impolite to ask for what one wanted which meant one could easily grow up to feel helpless and powerless. This kind of "good behavior" offered absolutely no experience in decision-making, and if these expectations were repeatedly enforced, they could create anger or feelings of being mistreated. It also leads to manipulative behavior because assertiveness would create guilt feelings.

I received many parental messages of this sort that were never meant to be destructive, but served to hamper my creativity and personal growth. Some of these messages to conform were antithetical to being a creative artist, musician, or writer. They hampered me to a certain extent, but I guess my creative impulses were too strong to be completely stifled. I often just "did my thing", but too often it was dampened with an awareness of what would be acceptable. I wasn't one to risk disapproval.

As a therapeutic antidote I visualized Miss Goody-two-shoes having a messy good time in the paints, and she ended her orgy of artful activity by going to the beach and digging sand with a shovel and putting it in a pail. That beach scene seemed rather inappropriate to me in terms of a healing, but she wanted to do it. Then I realized that it symbolic of what I really like to do which is digging for truth near the ocean of the collective conscious as well as of Spirit. The pail is also a container—a feminine symbol. Imagery of this type may need to be done over a period of time, and certainly if you catch the problem continuing or popping up occasionally.

As a counselor I frequently used imagery with women who were having similar problems in being assertive. These women often ended up meeting everyone else's needs and scarcely recognizing their own, much less being able to ask for what they wanted. When they did something for themselves they could easily feel undeserving and guilty. I "gave them permission" to address their own wants and needs. We learned what it meant to take responsibility for one's self and to how to make decisions. We talked about the difference between aggressiveness and assertiveness and the tendency to manipulate (even unconsciously) to get your own way if you can't be open about your needs or desires.

Imagining doing something so different from the way they ordinarily acted could be frightening at first. I would suggest they visualize building some kind of enclosure for protection if they felt threatened. I expected they would choose a wall or a castle. Imagine my surprise when one reported being in a paper bag and peering out at danger. Of course, this required changing to a place that offered more protection first, then she could imagine venturing out slowly after being convinced that she could call for help if need be. She could then practice asking for and receiving what she wanted; she also experienced being told "no" to discover that a refusal was not an earth-shaking event.

Another way would be to imagine being in charge of a group of people, she could be like an Army sergeant–give orders and see the group follow them. If she had difficulty doing that, she could stand on a chair or see the other people reduced to being smaller than she was. This exaggeration would introduce possibilities not previously recognized.

I simply opened a door to new ideas, and they discovered they were not punished for being "bad". We were forging new pathways in the brain.

Sometimes a vague fear is not recognized for what it is and may be experienced as shyness. Let me give you an example: a woman I worked with wanted to be able to make friends. She had a good job but never had experienced a lasting friendship, and she lived alone. She wanted to reach out and try to form some relationships, but had not had any success.

She entered counseling with the presenting problem of the inability to make and keep friends. She was helped to see that the vague anxiety she experienced was actually fear. She agreed to explore the problem with visualization.

I needed some place to start with the visualization, so I asked her to close her eyes and imagine going down a road. When I sensed she was comfortable with this, I suggested she ask for a symbol of her fear. She said she saw a tiger, and she was afraid. At this point I asked if she wanted to go ahead with it, and she said yes.

We sat quietly for a moment while I considered where I would go next. Before I decided on a question, she started laughing. I asked her what was funny, and she said, "I reached out to touch it and it turned into a little kitten."

We discovered that her fear was of rejection because she felt unlovable. This woman felt that her mother had never loved her; therefore, something must be wrong with her. She couldn't remember ever have been touched affectionately by her mother. She was very bitter about what she perceived as rejection.

In one session, she remembered hearing her mother say something nice about her while visiting across the fence with a neighbor. We used that memory as a first step to realizing that her mother did love her but was unable to express her feelings. Her mother was doing the best she could–her nurturing skills were so inadequate that we decided that she, herself, must have received poor mothering.

The client made progress from that point on, and finally was able to visit her mother for the first time in several years. She also started attending a study group where she was able to make friends with one of the members. Small steps lead to a healthier, more satisfying way to live for her.

The original break-through that came from the visualization was more rapid that usual. Most of the time I had to approach the symbol gingerly and ask many questions before reaching an answer, but the story illustrates the technique of using a symbol for the problem.

Let me give you another example of finding out what the problem actually is when it lies outside the client's awareness. I would ask that they be shown a symbol that would stand for the problem. The client may see for instance a rock on a path. I would then ask it to take human form so that I could converse with it. I would then ask its name, then to tell what was the problem. It usually turns out to be a part of self that had been overlooked, judged unworthy of existence, or condemned. We allow it to tell its story and listen to the griping, complaining, pleading or protesting for a while in order to let some of the energy that had been tied up in it dissipate. This also gives us a clearer picture of matter.

I am now switching over to having the client ask the questions for him or herself. They can do this in their mind and report back to me. I would have the client ask, "What do you want from me?" We are careful at this point because "want" can easily be the aspect of self that desires to take over completely and get its own way. They may well want to rule the roost; if this occurs, the client is to firmly tell it, "No." The client must always remember that they are the one who is in charge.

Then the next question is asked, "What do you need from me?" Need and want are different. "Need" is the bottom line. The answer will probably will be, "I need for you to recognize me; I am a part of you too. I need more time and attention—more space." This is reasonable and the client would agree.

If there are two opposing parts they need to dialogue, listen to each other's complaints and more or less make room for each other by compromising. Your role as client or as the one seeking a resolution to a problem is to comment or ask questions that will lead to a resolution. Once this become resolved I suggest they exchange gifts that are a symbol of their power. By doing so the client, or yourself as the case may be, will feel more in balance and more content.

Visualization can be helpful as a tool to practice accomplishing something you are afraid to do, or want to be able to do better. For instance, if you have something you dread doing, such as asking for a raise, or making a speech, you can walk through it successfully in your imagination over and over until your mind realizes you actually can do it. Start by letting the part that is afraid express his or her fear, then, dialogue with the opposite part. The one who wants to succeed may talk about wanting to achieve a goal, receive praise and attention, or simply want to improve his or her life.

When I first started using visualization, it was not commonly recognized or used. Now, many athletes regularly use visualization to mentally practice the perfect way to execute any movement they want to make such as a golf stroke, ski jump, or a skating routine. They see themselves doing it perfectly and succeeding. The golf ball drops into the hole, the skier effortlessly soars through the air and lands perfectly, the skater leaps gracefully and lands the jump smoothly. Sales people use another common practice; they mentally practice their sales pitch and see themselves making in the sale. You can discover potential in your imagination and overcome fears. In doing this, you also rid yourself of an unconscious belief that you are helpless or inadequate.

Use your imagination and practice being the person you would like to be. You can discover and practice what it means to be "up front" and a good communicator. Parents teach small children not to cross the street; an older child needs to be able to do so. You must, at times, do the forbidden thing in order to grow. Even if you fail in your first efforts, you learn that your mistakes are not fatal; you try again.

I taught Art to young students several years ago. I explained that we had to learn the rules of good drawing and painting, but that after we had learned those rules, we had to try breaking them—to experiment and be creative. In one Art class I took at UT, we were assigned just such a project. I was to paint a picture with the subject not centered and partly off the edge of the canvas. When I related this to one of my students, she listened solemnly and then said, "Mrs. McMaster, you don't strike me as the kind of person who breaks rules." I guess Miss-goody-two shoes must still show at times. She must be part of my shadow, darn it.

UNFOLDING

Don't shy away from me,
seeing my shortcomings,
that I present so gleefully.
I've dug deep
in that attic trunk
to retrieve
those parts of self
I packed away
amidst mothballs
of disapproval,
condemned by others
or by me.
They've been hostages imprisoned
through distorted expectations
and useless messages.
From their interment
I bring them forth,
expose them to the light,
and give them a flap
to smooth out the ridges
pressed by time.
Debris falls away
like so much dust,
revealing remnants of self
I had buried needlessly.
I welcome them with love
and set them free.

Chapter 7
Who You Are

Let us enlarge upon the concept of using meditation to help the personality unfold and be more balanced. Roberto Assagioli, an Italian doctor, was one of the early psychiatrists, and he formulated a concept called Psychosynthesis. He studied under Freud but became a follower of Carl Jung's. Freud did not believe in God, and Assagioli disagreed; he felt that the soul should be considered in psychology. Like Jung he felt that such attributes as creativity, altruism, and transpersonal feelings came from the unconscious mind and must be considered when addressing the personality. Freud formulated his concepts from his work with the mentally ill. Assagiolli worked with neurotics and was interested in teaching individuals to seek personal growth and expansion of consciousness.

Assagioli recognized the personality consisted of many different aspects and referred to them as sub-personalities. The ego is the director of the personality, but Assagioli believed in a Higher Self, or Soul, that lay outside of conscious awareness and was a human being's connection with Divine Mind. By learning to access this Higher Self, one could tap into a source of infinite wisdom that could furnish guidance and strength.

The ego, (or self spelled with a lower case letter), thinks it is the most important fixture of the personality, but it is often described as the "tip of the iceberg". The unconscious mind is much larger, but lies outside of our conscious awareness. The ego rushes to take credit for things that go well in the individual's life and easily becomes inflated with it's own importance. When anything goes wrong, it proclaims its innocence and quickly blames someone or something else. It is always interested in promoting and protecting itself. It can make unwise decisions because it fails to draw on the wisdom that is available through the Higher Self. It frequently overrides feelings or sensations that send warning signals that the ego's decision is flawed and will lead the personality in a wrong direction.

Sub-personalities are often related to the roles we are called upon to play such as daughter, wife, or mother, but they are more meaningful than the roles. They are the archetypal energy patterns described by Jung; he derived his material from myths that occur in different cultures. The patterns described by Assagioli are taken from familiar patterns found in our every day life. Some common ones are "rescuer", "martyr", "daddy's little princess", and "nurse". We can move in and out of these aspects of self, but generally speaking, they make up an adaptation to life— the way your personality expresses. Your adaptation tends to change from time to time during your life-journey.

Some sub-personalities are more active or more important than others are, and any of these can easily become dominant. For instance, when I was a graduate student, much of my time, energy, and my attention were invested in it; my future depended on my success However, in the sub-personality of student, I neglected playtime, feeling that it was unnecessary and that I should be using the time to study.

You can keep that going for a while, but if you ignore the opposing part that needs rest and recreation, you will hit a bad patch. At its worst, it could be called an identity crisis.

If you were to graph the activity of the opposing parts, a crisis would occur when the lines intersect. That would be the day when you wake up and something inside says, "My life feels empty. I can't keep going like this."

The part of you that wants to stay on the beach and the part that wants to work hard to be successful can easily engage in a tug of war. Listening to both sides of the story can break the strangle hold. The two will always exist within you. Life is designed that way to provide choices and to give you the opportunity to readjust and achieve balance.

An airplane flying from one city to another appears to take a straight path, but it actually must make constant course corrections to get there. Remember, when you are driving, you move the steering wheel frequently as you keep in your chosen lane.

Another thing that we should recognize is that the personality by its very nature is made up of opposites, and both sides need to be acknowledged. This causes internal disagreements because the sub-personalities can conflict with one another. One aspect may want to do "this" and opposes another one that wants to do "that". Ignoring one of them is dangerous because the one that is shut out can gather energy to burst upon the scene at a later date and take over, or it can hide in the shadows to sabotage the ego's choice with silent destructiveness.

Personality problems often arise because an aspect of self may have been judged to be unworthy, bad, sick, or stupid. Recognizing and dealing with this brings the personality back into balance and releases the energy tied up in the dysfunctional "hang up" to flow into personal growth.

Let's use a flower as a metaphor for the personality as a whole. The center of the flower could be seen as the ego, and petals cluster around it can be seen as sub-personalities. In nature, no one flower petal becomes abnormally large, but a sub-personality can take over because of its importance.

Assagioli is known for his premise that one can take one's sense of identity from a sub-personality instead of the personality as a whole. One sub-personality thinks it is the most important and can dominate others, for instance, when a woman thinks of herself as "mother" and doesn't do anything to take care of her own needs. She may even feel guilty taking time away from home. Professional people often take their identity from their specialty.

One of the easiest example is that of being a doctor. Ask who they are and they probably will answer, "I'm a doctor". What about the part of self that would rather stay home more and enjoy family life? Much money, effort, and experience has been invested in the becoming the competent professional, and so much depends on maintaining it that it easily becomes the only thing that matters to the person involved and to the members of the family.

I will present an exercise that can bring the personality back into balance later in this chapter, but first I need to discuss the development of a "fair witness", or "impartial observer". The fair witness is unlike the sub personalities in that it needs to be developed through imagination. This is the aspect of self that stands aside and assesses what is going on in order to break the hold of a dominating aspect of self and can clearly evaluate the problem. This peacemaker not only can bring conflict to resolution, it can provide access to wisdom and spiritual guidance to the personality.

The "fair witness" or "impartial observer" lies outside the configuration of the personality in order not to get caught up with the machinations of the ego. When the fair witness recognizes that a sub-personality is dominating, it listens to the dialogue of opposing parts and provides a solution. This compromise meets their needs at least to some extent. Recognizing and listening to the argument will relieve tension and allows movement to a better position. Without the help of the fair witness a person can make unwise choices during such a crisis. Tempered with wisdom, a change of direction that is not destructive can be a better choice.

In instances where only one sub-personality is involved the fair witness can provide answers to questions and give advice. The witness speaks the Truth. It is thought to be our connection with Divine Mind.

Some people may feel more comfortable speaking of a Higher Power rather than speaking of God or Divine Mind. However, in the end it makes no difference what name you choose, the Creator has been creating long before you came into this world, and will do so long after you cease to be. Denying its existence is foolish arrogance, and it also means that you are cutting yourself off from the inner peace and wisdom that comes from knowing the Truth. The Creator is far more powerful than any of us can ever comprehend. The Source of Life created you, and you are a part of it. This means you are able to draw upon that energy and on Infinite Wisdom for guidance. The fair witness is separate from the parts of self. You can use the symbolism of a wise old woman or man. In meditation, ask for this person to appear and take whatever pops into your mind, no matter what gender. It is helpful to see the fair witness situated at a higher level above the two who are in disagreement. A pronouncement by the fair witness coming from the third position keeps you from becoming caught in the polarity.

Assagioli teaches that taking ones identity from a sub-personality means being identified with it. The fair witness enables one to "dis-identify" with it and free the energy that can then create a healthier personality.

Any time you catch yourself thinking of a sub-personality as who you are, you can take back control instead of letting it run your life. Becoming dis-identified with it means you can feel the sensation of being centered and in charge of your life. At this point Assagioli teaches that one must use will power to grow and unfold more of one's potential. He provided an exercise to develop will power because this is needed to move from the resolutions reached in meditation to the outer reality and be able to set and reach goals. If you find yourself reacting to the word "will" in a negative way, it is because you are thinking of will as something being imposed upon you by some one who wants to dominate and control you. Assagioli differentiates between the will that is used to overpower someone else and the will that empowers the individual to accomplish his or her goal. This is the will to accomplish what you want to achieve.

***

I encountered the wise old person again when I later took part in a workshop for professionals given in Austin,

Texas that appeared in a workshop for therapists that I attended. It was given by highly credentialed therapist using Psychosynthesis , and he led us through a series of guided meditations to demonstrate Assagioli's roadmap of the personality.

The leader of the guided meditation said: "Think of yourself as being seated at a round table. This is a board meeting, and you are the chairman of the board. Seated around the table are parts of self. These are your sub-personalities, and they serve as members of the board. Carefully observe them and note who is in attendance."

After we had done this, he changed the scene: "The board meeting has ended and you have gone on a holiday. See yourself out in the country seated under a shady tree in a comfortable lawn chair, feet propped up, and sipping a cold drink. Your tranquility is interrupted when you see cloud of dust arising on the horizon. Soon you can see a bus headed toward you. It comes to a stop in front of you. The door opens, and the characters that comprise your board tumble out and gather together into a group and begin a discussion. Then they get into an argument. A wise old person is standing on the ledge at a slightly higher elevation above the people, and they decide to ask this wise old person to solve their argument. They present a question and wait for an answer. Instantaneously the answer to that question popped into my head.

I attended this workshop many years ago, and unfortunately, I don't remember what I asked the wise old person, but I do remember that I had hardly finished wording my question when the answer came, and this astounded me.

Looking back on the experience I remember that at first my sub-personalities had appeared indistinctly–I had a little trouble envisioning my board of directors. However, the images soon became more clear and definitive as we got deeper into meditation. I felt relaxed and peaceful as I saw myself being on vacation; I was enjoying being alone. I felt annoyed that my quiet peacefulness was to be interrupted by the workshop leader describing what was taking place.

One interesting side-note is that the bus neared me from the right, but when it pulled up in front of me and started unloading it arrived from the left meaning that the direction had reversed and had changed into a counter-clockwise movement. (Material from the unconscious often presents in a counter-clockwise manner.)

I experienced a surprise when those people tumbled rapidly out of the bus because my artist-self, dressed in a painting smock with brushes and palette in hand, exited by walking over the heads of the others. I hadn't even seen her at the board meeting.

The goal of the meditation was to demonstrate a way to retrieve information from the unconscious mind, but it had an added dimension for me because I not only received an answer to my question, I found my artist self. I hadn't been painting for quite a while, although I had drawn and painted since I was a small child. She was still present waiting for me to once again recognize her existence.

The persistent artist sub-personality formed out of being the only child in an artistic family; I was taught and learned to entertain myself at an early age by drawing and painting. If I had not recognized her in this meditation, she would probably have found her way into expression sooner or later.

When she surfaced I didn't have time to visit with her because I had to go on with the directions given to the group, but if I were to encounter an overlooked sub-personality while meditating by myself, I would engage it in conversation. The artist might have felt devalued by my not seeing her at the table. She probably would have said, "You didn't remember me! You don't think I'm important? Don't you realize I am a gift? My feelings are hurt."

My role in the dialogue would be one of attempting to repair that wound. I would try to reassure her and tell her she would always be an important part of my life, and from now on I would try to let her be more active. In a case where conflict is not the issue, I will always seek harmony, personal growth and balance. The object in working in this manner is to seek wholeness of self.

The way these sub-personalities can conflict became apparent in the next exercise that we did in this workshop. The leader asked the participants to make a list of things they wanted out of life. We then gathered in groups of five. From these you picked the top four desires in terms of importance. Each one of us took a turn sitting in the center of the circle. You assign one statement to each of the four other members of your small group and they are to verbalize simultaneously while you sit in the center with eyes closed, and listening.

Hearing this din was confusing, and I had a hard time letting go to let the process happen; that caused me to stay longer in the center than the others before experiencing the resolution of the conflict. Finally, two messages faded from my hearing while the two remaining voices became loud and clear. The conflict was between a part that wanted to work hard and become very successful and another part that warned me not to work too hard or I might get sick. This "take it easy" message emanated from my mother, who believed one should rest and not work too hard because getting tired endangered one's health. This had arisen out of her experience of being so ill and being told to rest which she, in turn, taught me.

This was the last of the exercises in that workshop. In that brief stretch of time the leader had managed to cover almost completely the heart of Assagioli's work— the sub-personalities—the concept of the fair witness who, incidentally, could be seen as one's own High Self.

***

Once you start your inner explorations you discover your own particular sub-personalities, and they are always fascinating. One of the ones I discovered in the process of self-examination during meditation was "Brunhilda". When looking at old notes, I discovered I had been so intrigued with her that I had written about my negotiations with her many years ago.

I wrote, "Much like a Wagnerian soprano, she stood with spear in hand; she wore a Viking horned headpiece, and her breasts were protected by round, brass covers. She was large and her attitude was one of complete stubbornness. Once having chosen to defend her territory, there would be no moving her."

I learned from Brunhilda that she resisted manipulation simply by resistance. She was highly developed because I wasn't skilled at confrontation or negotiating differences. She was an outgrowth of the many messages I received as a child that I should not express my anger but should be sweet and always behave nicely.

Brunhilda was, indeed, a fine discovery. What strength she had! A pro football lineman would never move her. I certainly didn't have to worry about taking care of myself. She had been there all the time and I hadn't recognized her. What irony—I resisted being controled by controlling!

Blessings always have another side; I realized she never intended to compromise or to relinquish her hold, and this could be counterproductive. My negotiations therefore took on a new tone. "Brunhilda," I said, "I really appreciate your strength and your dedication to duty, but you must allow yourself to let go when need be." However, this was like trying to retrieve a juicy steak bone from a large, hungry dog. She had no intention of giving up her domain. I decided she would have to expend her energy in a different way. I encouraged her to rant and rage. She loved it. She would do a war dance ceremoniously declaring her superiority.

Firm measures had to be taken. I addressed her sternly: "Brunhilda, you will mind. You will sit yourself down over there. I am in charge here. If you don't do as I say, I'll have to shrink you down until you are very small." Grumbling, she conceded and sat on a chair in disgust.

We exchanged gifts as usual at the end of the session. I knew my work with Brunhilda was completed when I received an astounding gift from her. I asked for a gift that represented her strength. Much to my complete amazement and amusement, I saw the image of one of her hubcap-like brass bosom coverings being presented to me. Somewhat repulsed, I flashed back, "I don't want that thing!" Undaunted, this round, conical shaped thing instantly turned over and became a receptacle containing a beautiful bouquet of flowers!

Her gift meant that because she was available for my protection; without her insistence on control, I could let my guard down and could therefore be more receptive—a feminine trait. Remember–any container can be a symbol for the feminine.

Another important aspect of myself that I discovered was Flapper. She was curvaceous, provocative, and she batted her eyes when she assumed her best, seductive stance. Since she had curly hair, she would quickly fluff it up with her hand anytime she felt recognized or desired. She was embarrassing, to say the least, and was an outgrowth of being Daddy's little princess.

When I discovered her, I tried to get rid of her and sent her to a deserted island for early retirement. I saw her with feet propped up on an ottoman and she was sipping a mint julep. That didn't work well; she didn't like being retired. Then I discovered that she had a lot of charm, a wicked sense of humor, and had aided in the success of many ventures because there was so much life in her. I brought her back out of retirement after reaching an understanding with her about her behavior.

She behaved, but the spirit was still there. When she is attracted to something or someone, she is still inclined to go into her dance, but her dance grew much more subdued and short-lived as I grew older. Instead of condemning her, I learned to recognize her existence and appreciate her liveliness. I had a choice about whether I acted on her desires.

Another sub-personality, my inner critic, was strong; she is quick to try to run the show and has a well-developed forefinger lengthened from pointing. Her name was Percy–short for Persnickity, and her lips puckered like a draw string purse when she was into being disdainfully "right". She likes to blame others, but often it is I who receives her condemnation, and that can be lethal. I see her as angular; her clothes don't lie in soft folds, but make sharp angles where they must bend. I was ready to guillotine her until I realized she was my editor when writing and helped give balance and accuracy to my painting because she can discern anything that is out of kilter. She demonstrates the fact that every part of self has value—the attractive as well as the less-than-desirable aspect.

**

Assagiol's "Who Am I" exercise to help you become centered and balanced follows:

To think of yourself in terms of your career, your attractive appearance, your youth, the way you dress, or your wealth, or what you own, is to invest a lot of importance in something transient and incomplete. Beauty fades; styles are popular today, dated tomorrow. Objects break, rust, or wear out, careers can fail, and there are many ways to lose your wealth. When this happens, who will you be?

As much as it pleases us to have qualities or things that are desirable, they don't have the ability to make us feel complete. Some morning we may wake up and realize that what we have held so dear isn't the key to happiness. If you have taken your identity from what you do or have, you have diminished yourself. You simply haven't answered the question in depth.

Who are you? Who is there when you when you wake up in the middle of the night?

Sit in a comfortable position and close you eyes. Take your thoughts off the outer world and focus inward. When you feel quiet and relaxed, imagine moving inward until you reach the very center of your being.

Silently say: "I have a body. My body is subject to change. I can be sick; I can be well. I gain weight; I lose weight. I am more than my body." Contemplate that for a few moments, and then add, "I am a child of God. I am a center of pure consciousness."

Expand that by using other aspects of your beingness: "I have a brain. My brain can be active, and or my brain can be idle. I am more than my brain. I have thoughts, but they change. My thoughts race at times, and are slow at times." After a few moments add, "I have a career, but I am more than my career. My career may change over time, but the I am of me will last for as long as I live. My career is part of my life. It is transitory and its importance and its stability may vary. I am more than that. My career is something I do; it is valuable, but I am more than my career. I am a child of God, a creation of Divine Mind, a center of pure consciousness, and that fact will never change."

When you feel you have accomplished this task, give thanks for your success and retrace your steps until you have reached your starting place. Slowly open your eyes and return your awareness to the outer reality.

Just saying these words will begin the process that brings you into better balance. Feeling "centered" is a word often used today, but it only came into usage in recent years, and I think it came out of the experience of meditation. This exercise creates a centered feeling. You will have dis-identified with, and are no longer possessed by any aspect of self. You are centered, rather than being out of balance, and you are now in control and can make wise decisions about your life.

This exercise is particularly successful in getting hold of addictions. I presented Assagioli's Roadmap to the Personality at a large conference on alcoholism in Houston, and this workshop received the highest rating. The aspect of self that is addicted has taken possession of the personality in the sense that it has overwhelmed the part of self that would choose to be healthy. The fair witness listens to a discussion (more like an argument) between the two and the addicted one is heard but is refused the right to rule.

Alcoholics Anonymous is more successful than any approach in treating addiction, and Assagioli's recognition of a Higher Self fits in neatly with its approach. Even if your problem is being too fond of chocolate, this meditative exercise can be of help.

THE SOURCE

Deep within
my inner spaces
lies the center
of my being,
life created
by Spirit Source,
welling up
and flowing forth,
expressing my
potential self.

Let any walls
I've built of fear
be carried away
by the life current,
healing, forming,
unrestricted,
lest my uniqueness
be diminished.

Mind-Body-Spirit,
be balanced, centered.
Express as I am
meant to be.

Chapter 8
The Turning Point

Marriage counseling was a large part of my practice while I was in the mental health field, but I never encountered a divorce more traumatic than my own. Probably many divorced people feel that way, but for years afterward, I would begin shaking when I spoke of it. Leaving was a drastic step for me because, like so many women of that era, I "didn't have permission" to ask for what I wanted and felt powerless when challenged.

I had recognized that for the sake of my own well being, I had to extricate myself, and it was a long, painful process. No divorce is easy, especially when children are involved. I tried valiantly to keep them from becoming embroiled in it, but to no avail. Every possible tactic was used in an attempt to get me to return to the marriage, but having finally gotten the courage to leave, I would never have returned. It took me a year to get into court, and I achieved this after learning to persist and to be more forceful.

The trauma of that divorce caused me to feel alienated from God. The experience shook my faith. I assumed the label "agnostic" because I simply didn't know where the truth lay and struggled on with my life. Despite my questions, I never stopped believing–never called myself an atheist. However, I did believe in my exclusion from His family, and that was a very lonely place to be.

In those days a divorced person felt a total failure, very different and very alone. After a while, I realized that I was angry with God. How could He do this to me? I met this dilemma with the equipment I often used–withdrawal because I felt hurt and powerless, and I pouted. This would surely show God the great injustice He had done. Maybe He would recognize His mistake, and somehow remedy the problem.

The accepted way to explain a divorce at that time was to go into a litany of how terrible the situation was, why one needed to get out of the marriage, and how hard one had tried to save it. Blame is such an easy weapon to use, but it impels every one from relatives to friends to take sides. The worst damage is done to children when one parent tries to convince children that the other is the cause of the breakup.

Blaming others is never the answer. It invites defensiveness and retaliation. It solves no problems; it brings no comfort. Blame causes alienation, and is destructive to everyone involved. Most importantly, it does not facilitate movement to another level of consciousness that would offer a better way of life.

The cause of a break-up is never the fault of just one of the partners; each plays a role in the failure of that marriage, and the resulting guilt gnawed at me for a long time. At the time, however, I had no idea what role I had played that helped lead to its demise. My own defense mechanisms would not allow me to see my contribution to the dysfunction of the marriage.

When anyone goes through a rough spot, or a tragedy in life, the solution lies in taking responsibility for your part of the problem by asking how you either contributed to or helped cause the problem. The answer may well be a resolution rather than a solution, but one can only grow from the experience if it is faced honestly rather than distorted. This also allows reparation of the relationships with those involved. This doesn't mean self-blame, which would just be the opposite of blaming the other.

An effective way of doing this is to become the observer—the fair witness—and discover when and why the thing went astray. Only then can you discover your own contribution to the problem. Doing this gives you the opportunity to repair the damage or simply use the information as an instrument for personal growth. Both partners are involved in that dysfunctional dance.

Looking back on it, I had unconsciously assumed the role of the innocent victim. It wasn't a role I chose; I thoroughly believed I was a victim. I didn't put down the children's father to them, however. I had enough good judgment not to do that, but I did let everyone who loved me see my view. Such a standpoint was understandable because of the culture in which we lived. A woman's role had been proscribed by society; we were supposed to be nice, and serve others even to the point of being self-sacrificing. That stance leaves no room for asking for what one wants or standing up for what one believes to be right.

At that time point in time, I couldn't define the problem much less have any sense of how to bring about change. I had no negotiating tools, no power that I recognized.

Besides that, by the time I found the courage to leave, I would not have considered working on a solution. I was in a different place entirely.

To this day, I am appalled when I see this pattern enacted by others in my viewing. Most often I see it in older women who became stuck in that old way of being. I feel angry because I know how destructive it is to the person who is not taking responsibility for their life and to the relationship that has to be deteriorating. I react in anger because it reminds me of my own past destructive behavior. Older women are not the only ones who do this, however; anyone who is into blame instead of claiming his or her own role, whatever happens, is not living in a mature manner and is blocking their chance at personal growth. Forgiveness is fine, but it shouldn't be given in a blindness that buries the causal problems or it will return.

It is possible to unravel the problems in a relationship before they snarl into a hopeless knot if they are addressed soon enough. Marriage counseling can do wonders if each partner is willing to look at his or her role in the situation and is willing to change. It is doomed to failure if the relationship has eroded into bitterness and one or both of the partners doesn't want to try. Conscious or unconscious resistance dooms counseling to failure when either partner regards the marriage as an intolerable situation.

At first, I couldn't understand what had occurred between us. Time had to pass before I could pull my nose away from the tree trunk and discover the forest. When I did this, I discovered that my idea of how to be a good wife evolved from observing my parental family as well as from societal norms.

I had always thought of my parents as being a loving couple, and during my childhood their love for one another

made me see their marriage as ideal. This was largely due to
the fact that they didn't fight—at least not in front of me.
The family operated in a peaceful manner, and I knew that
I was loved and that I was treated well by my parents. I had
not recognized the lack of any avenue to discuss differences.
As a matter of fact differences were not even recognized
and certainly not discussed or issues resolved.

Anger was an absolute no-no. My mother's anxiety
would begin to rise at the least hint that someone might not
like or agree with what was taking place. I realize now that
this must have been related to her position in her parental
family, having been born a few days before her father died.
Her position must have felt tenuous since her birth was
so linked to the loss of the head of that household—the
deeply loved husband and father. At any rate, I had learned
that misbehavior was unacceptable, and anger was to be
buried rather than expressed in any manner.

As a teenager I rebelled against her over-protectiveness
and became, for a short while, a tyrant—at least in small
increments. It did foster a kind of stubbornness in me
that became a determined independence that proved to be
valuable. I also learned to be secretive about my misbehavior,
and that probably served me well in the atmosphere in
which I lived.

Years later, when I was a therapist and used dream
analysis in my work, my mother casually told me of a
dream she'd had. It's meaning was so clear to me that I
couldn't imagine why she could not see and understand
it. However, she reported it with her usual naiveté. In her
dream the television set was covered with volcanic ash.
With the faultless perfection of dream symbolism, the ash
was that buried unexpressed anger that interfered with
meaningful communication within the family. The ash

obscured the picture on the screen; it had lost its capacity to burn, but still smoldered. I felt sad about that, but made no comment. It wasn't my place to analyze my mother's dream. I thought it was too late to point out the existence of Vesuvius. Besides, I was too well trained to break the "don't recognize it" rule.

My parents had been molded by years of meeting each other's expectations. The protrusions of their individuality had eroded by the demands of conformity as they faced the vicissitudes of life with bravery and determination. They loved each other to the end, but what a price they paid.

It wasn't until I became a counselor that I realized being a good wife involved more than being compliant. In my own marriage my husband's flaws had been obvious, mine less recognizable, so I had concluded that I was the good one. There are always two sides to every problem and it takes two to tango.

***

After the divorce and my loss of faith, I wandered in the desert of agnosticism for ten or fifteen years, and believe me, that desert can be mighty hot and dusty. I wandered around, danced with Gila monsters and concentrated on getting an education.

I occasionally went to a church, the choice of denomination being decided by curiosity. The impetus arose from loneliness; my alienation would not have lasted as long if parishioners had welcomed me, but my own reticence kept that from happening. I felt so unacceptable that I created my isolation. I wanted to be welcomed but didn't take the initiative and was ignored. Members of the

Episcopalian church I happened to choose were still into their "frozen chosen" role, and I didn't return.

My interest in the Spiritual was betrayed by the fact that I studied Philosophy of Religion while attending the University of Texas. However, those were also the days when I was into my pseudo-intellectual mode. I was stuck in a left-brain mentality. Examined by reason, such things as miracles made no sense at all.

A professor who taught Philosophy of Religion had once been a priest but had left the priesthood because he had come to feel that no one denomination had all the answers or owned exclusive right to the Truth. He was a small man of Italian descent, and he tended to stride up and down waving his arms as he lectured unwittingly sowing the seeds of a faith in Spirit that might sprout later in our lives.

A change occurred in my own belief system when I learned to meditate in the late sixties. Both my children, who were then young adults, had learned to meditate and inspired me to attend a class. I learned by using a mantra that served as a tool for focusing. At our final class, we ceremoniously spent the allotted time sitting quietly and saying our mantra. Our teacher announced that we had passed the course; we had now meditated. But nothing earth-shaking occurred. I felt very peaceful, but had I really gotten into a meditative state? I questioned that, but kept practicing, and after meditating on a regular basis for a while I found myself looking forward to and enjoying that period of quietness. I also found that this is the place where you discover the truth about anything, yourself included. The wonderful function performed at this level of consciousness is that the differing sides of any conflict can become reconciled, and the core of the matter resolves into middle ground that is accompanied by a "peace that passes all understanding".

Meditation opened a door that I had shut a long time ago. It was as if Spirit was just waiting for an opportunity to enter my consciousness. It didn't happen in a dramatic flash during meditation; it came in a series of dreams and a couple of extraordinary experiences that I will share with you.

WHEN ITS TIME FOR GRIEVING

I awaken.
The mass of heaviness inside
demands to speak,
having waited patiently
through a day
spent ministering
to other people's pain.
The hours had blindly bumped
against the edges of routine
until the terminal of night
was reached.
Then denial presented
its inflated claim
to my exhausted body,
and sleep intervened.
The heavy lump
waited only a brief time,
then insisted
that I wake and listen.
"Don't you remember?
Something precious died today."

Chapter 9
Revelatory Dreams And Synchronistic Events

We sat around the kitchen table casually talking that night—two psychologists and I—pontificating on life and what we believed. My husband of that time period was a devout atheist, and I had declared myself to be an agnostic. When we married no points of disagreement regarding our belief systems rubbed rough edges. His disbelief didn't bother me because of my own doubts.

This was a second marriage. That first marriage had ended in divorce after eighteen years. To that time my religious belief consisted of an unquestioning acceptance of what I had been taught as a child. After the trauma of the divorce, I had lost faith.

The truth was that I had failed in marriage and was disappointed in myself. Going through life without taking charge of your self doesn't work well, and if you don't see yourself as being in charge, you haven't truly accepted responsibility for your life. I had assumed "happily ever after" was a given and didn't recognize one's need to work at a relationship.

Years passed before I recognized that my anger at God prevented me from recognizing my own contribution to the demise. The passage of time spent in college did nothing to solve this problem; it simply evolved into a left-brain kind of rational questioning of religion in general that left me with an embittered skepticism. I decided that the God concept didn't make sense.

I had later moved to thinking of God as a creative energy, but that wasn't very satisfying and certainly offered no comfort when it was needed. Our discussion that night, however, served to clarify my thoughts; I had inadvertently dug down to discover a bedrock of belief in God that had always existed deep within me. I recently found notes that recounted that conversion written the following day, and it ended with the statement, "I know there is a creative force at work in this universe, but I do not know his name." This may sound like just another affirmation of my agnosticism, but it was more than that; it was an admission that I believed in something larger than myself was at work here.

The other agnostic in the conversation had agreed with me. How arrogant we were, but I didn't realize it at the time. It now reminds me of a flea riding on an elephant's back saying, "I think something is transporting me."

My recognition of God's existence, no matter how inadequate it was, apparently opened the door to Spirit. That night I had the first of a series of dreams that appeared over a period of time. The first presented a simple story expressing the eternal presence of the creator and invited me to understand more about the whole of life. The overall theme didn't center on me as an individual as much as it was a story that stretched across time to present an eternal truth.

Scene 1. I am in a brilliant azure sky and suddenly I am falling, but a long, flowing weeping willow branch adorned with spring-green leaves appears beside me, and I grasp it. I am lowered gently into a small boat that keeps me safe from the vast sea.

Scene 2. I am now standing on a pier. Connecting to the pier is a bin filled with garments of various kinds; they don't appear to be new. I have the feeling they have been worn many times. I am to pick something out to wear.

Scene 3. I find myself in a huge warehouse filled with shelves that reach to the ceiling, each laden with very large books. I reach up for one and pull it out.

Falling from the sky, I believe pictured the important change that occurred when I fell out of my inflated position of questioning the existence of my maker to my affirmation of God's existence. Like all changes, it created fear. What does it mean—what lies ahead?

I remember the brilliance of the sky and the chartreuse leaves of the weeping willow branch that expressed a beautiful world rather than a dangerous one. the colors disappear with the sea scene. I believe the absence of color signified that this is pre-conscious material entering my mind—the unknown is being revealed by the dream.

The sea symbolizes the unconscious mind or universal consciousness. The boat kept me from being overwhelmed by this powerful force. The pier would be connected to earth and provide the stable grounding of a different way of understanding.

The clothes could represent a change of adaptation to life–possibly a past life, a different way of being me and an evolution in my understanding of my world. They had been worn previously, and when I awakened, I felt they symbolized past lives. I happen to believe in reincarnation because I have had dreams about past lives, and it makes sense to me that energy doesn't die, but rather it reforms. We may come back again and again to learn what we need to learn.

This would tie into the presence of the storehouse, or library, which I believe to be the Akashic records which are an imagined spiritual realm supposedly holding a record of all events, actions, thoughts and feelings. In this case, I don't remember selecting a particular book because the dream ended here. However, I believe that any book I took out would contain a record of my own past lives–my own history so to speak. The fact that I didn't take one out may simply indicate that my understanding was incomplete or that was not what was important to the dream. The dream message spoke of the presence of a continuing creative force that has existed throughout eternity.

A human being's vision of life evolves out of their experiences within their environment. From this, they decide what the world is like. Changes occur as time goes on, yet to me the dream says that this lifetime is not all there is; it is infinitely more expansive and meaningful than we can even imagine.

These dream scenes impacted my consciousness; I felt shaken when I awoke the next morning. I recognized their importance, but I also knew my understanding was limited.

Other dreams would follow and during that time, I had two peak experiences. This type of synchronistic event far exceeds smaller incidences that surprise us with their unexpected nature; they are so profound that they cause a tremendous feeling of shock. Material from the unconscious breaks through into consciousness and the energy required to fuel the experience is powerful. These events are rare and are unforgettable. The shock that accompanies synchronicity can be profound and leaves you feeling like you have suddenly been thrust into a totally different dimension or reality in some inexplicable way.

At the time these occurred, we were living out in the country, and for some reason I was not going into work that day. I was alone and with absolutely no expectation of my privacy being interrupted. As far as I knew, no one was anywhere in the vicinity.

The back porch of the house was a covered area with comfortable chairs that clustered near the swimming pool. A hanging basket filled with a plant hung from the porch ceiling, and it needed water. I filled a pitcher with water, went out onto the porch and pulled a chair close to the basket. I climbed up on it and stood precariously perched there and started to pour. Suddenly a frantic chirping alerted me to the fact that I was about to flood a cardinal's nest tucked unwisely within the greenery. Three tiny pink birds responded to the intrusive pitcher spout by eagerly opening their beaks in expectation of a nice worm gift from momma; they didn't realize their home was in danger of being flooded. At that moment, a memory flashed into my mind of something a client had said the previous day. He had quoted from Herman Hess's <u>Damian</u>, "The bird must destroy one world in order to fly free to God."

In a complete state of shock, I went back into the house, and emptied the water from the pitcher into the sink. I went to my bedroom and plopped into an easy chair to contemplate what had happened. However, almost instantly an added shock occurred. I was seated close to another door that opened onto the porch, and it suddenly swung open. A black hand was on the doorknob and a black arm stretched out to reveal Willie, the man who took care of the yard and who was working that day unknown to me. For some reason he had opened the door. I thought that I was completely alone and this intrusion terrified me.

At that moment I mentally heard the words, "Don't be afraid". That offered comforting reassurance, but my sense of shock was actually intensified. To say I was jarred doesn't do it justice. I had never experienced anything even similar. My reality had been completely altered, and what could be more frightening than such an unexpected event and such a feeling of profound change?

Less dramatically than the synchronistic events, the dreams relentlessly continued, as if reinstating my change of consciousness. The next dream was more explicit than its predecessor. A circular pattern of scenes appeared and the first one began at the position of 6:30 o'clock:

Scene 1. I am seated in an auditorium type seat facing away from the center of a circle. A man is seated to my right.

Scene 2. The scene changes and the man is no longer present. I have now moved counterclockwise to approximately a 12:15 position. An old woman is seated to my right. She instructs me, "You have taken off your shoes, but you haven't removed your socks."

Scene 3. In the following scene, she is not present, and I am no longer seated but am facing inward toward the center of the circle. I am observing a group of people garbed in colorful outfits who have come from distant lands. They are seated on risers, and I know they are taking part in a religious ceremony of some kind.

Scene 4. In the last scene a gold cross hangs in a magenta sky in the area slightly to the left of 12:00 o'clock. An ornamentation adorns the intersection where the arms cross, making it unique.

To me, the man in the first scene symbolizes the left-brain intellectual way of thinking that is absent in the next scene as I turn inward to experience my spiritual feelings. The wise old woman is the proverbial inner guide who is to help me discover my standpoint, my understanding of life and the significance of my heritage.

I am becoming aware of a Higher Power, something larger than my self, yet I know I am being shown that I have a distinct and unique place within this all-encompassing presence. The gathering of diverse people worshipping together said to me that a belief in God is common to all cultures although it may be expressed in different ways.

The cross tells me that my ancestors were Christians, and the decoration at the cross section symbolizes the individuality of my heritage—like the sign of a clan or tribe. That heritage is infinitely more valuable to me than my claim to individuality and my right question. However,

I don't think of my questioning as having been sinful. God gave us a mind and curiosity; to use it is not bad, but my life would surely be diminished if I denied my birthright or the Truth. I would have been cutting myself of from my own root system.

The next dream spoke of my situation at that time:

> *I am in my own home, but it is dark and empty. I smell something sour. I say to my husband, "I smell something sour, and it's coming from the outside of the house next to our bedroom. Water must be there; let's go dig in the ground, then we will find the water and we'll get rid of the odor. My husband answers, "It can't be done."*

The dark emptiness of my home symbolized my soul without the enlightenment of spiritual belief. Water is a symbol of Spirit, and in the dream the water lies buried on the other side of the bedroom wall at the very point where the bed sits. It is "walled off"—separated from the bed where the masculine and feminine come together in the creative act. That also meant that I was asleep to the presence of God. So, once again, we see the theme of the masculine, left-brain intellect being unable to understand what the right is saying.

The dreams shorten after this and were less intricate, as if saying there is nothing left of the message that you haven't heard. Having covered the past and shown me the significance of my heritage, the dreams focused on my understanding of the present.

I have ridden across the entire nation on a LEM, the vehicle designed to ride on the moon. My husband is driving, and I am in a state of awe at what I have seen. Suddenly a large rabbit appears in the tall weeds to our left. For an instance I am frightened, but realize the rabbit is not dangerous. I excitedly turn to face my husband to tell him to look at the rabbit, and I realize that he is staring ahead with unseeing eyes. He has not seen anything of the wonders that I have seen during the entire trip.

In the dream I was riding on a high seat on the LEM, reminiscent of the "shotgun seat" on an old stagecoach, however the vehicle was definitely of modern construction. This meant I was high and in the open, which allowed me to see things clearly. It is interesting to note that the LEM was created especially for exploring the moon, which is symbolic of the feminine. Any vehicle symbolizes the energy that carries one through life and its strangeness would symbolize my new adaptation. Perhaps the fact that I am not driving illustrates the lack of importance of left-brain activity while in the dream state; he was not involved.

The rabbit is a symbol of creativity and creativity is a function of the right brain. I "knew" that in the dream we had traveled across the entire United States, however it seemed totally uninhabited. This is difficult to express, but it seemed to me that this indicated a natural state, free of man-made constructions—a basic truth.

Another brief dream occurred on a night soon afterward. In it I was looking at an apartment.

Scene 1. The entire décor of the apartment was pure white. I move through the rooms and find some green bushes in one of them. I call out in enthusiasm to unseen friends who are with me.

Scene 2. I enter a room with walls and ceiling constructed entirely of mirrors. In one corner the wall and the ceiling meet and bring together arcs of a pattern etched in glass causing a circular design to emerge. I call to my friends to come and see. They don't seem to be there, I am alone but feel like somehow they've made it possible for me to be there, and I decide to rent the apartment.

Scene 3. I see a green billfold opened and with many bills of large denominations fanning out from it. It is enough to provide anything I need or want, and I know I can afford to live in this apartment.

One last, brief dream brought an end to the entire series like a period at the end of a sentence.

I see a green Christmas tree with a cardinal perched like an ornament at the very top. Then I hear the words, "I believe".

What a fitting conclusion. A tree is a symbol for "the tree of life"; the cardinal is the symbol of my astrological sign of Aries, my birth sign. The color red is strong and powerful. In short, I have experienced a rebirth of major proportions; my life has changed. The apartment is a new place and something that I have chosen.

I am starting life anew with a clean slate; I am reconciled with God. It is a purely individual thing yet the remembrance of my mother and my heritage is present and my life is filled with abundance.

A while later when this rebirth had become more solid, I had a dream that summarized the process.

Scene 1. I am walking down a road and on my right is an expanse of buildings that are no longer standing; they are in shambles. I curve to my left and see a two-story building is standing there. On the second level, up high, I see three, small, stained glass windows grouped together. I think they are beautiful; I resolve to find the owner in order to buy them. However, I seem to find substitutes that are plastic; I reject them.

Scene 2. I am in a large ballroom. Many people are there. I observe this scene. A couple comes out on a balcony overlooking the ballroom and at the far end of the room. On the balcony a wedding takes place. Suddenly a small child is hanging by her knees on the balcony railing. Her dress has fallen away to reveal her body. I feel uncomfortable with this and move on.

Scene 3. I find myself in a home that is underground, buried beneath rich brown earth. Within it the walls are painted a cream color, and there is a raised decorative pattern on the wall; it is wood carved like a tree branch curved into a circle. This also is painted a cream color.

The effect is lovely and it seems valuable and an antique. A real estate agent is present and makes a bid to buy it. He offers a large sum of money, and I am pleased and surprised at the value of the home.

Scene 4. I am walking further; to my left I see a scene as if displayed for me. Three very large stained glass windows standing side by side form the background to the scene and in front of them is my grandmother's large, old, sturdy oak rocking chair.

I didn't realize at first that the dream scene formed an oval. It did not show my entire life, but depicted the conclusion of one adaptation and the beginning of a new way of being that heralded the discovery and claiming of my belief in the trinity. The old way of being was symbolized by the area that lay in ruin. I turn to find a higher state of consciousness depicted by the three small stained glass windows that I want to buy. Perhaps the fact that they were plastic represents my first limited acceptance of a higher power when I thought of it simply as energy. I didn't "buy" that idea but moved on.

The ballroom would represent universal consciousness and I am observing it but am not caught up in it; I have moved into a more individualized state of consciousness. The balcony would represent a higher way of being and the marriage would show the masculine and the feminine principle joining to form a more whole personality. The child hanging from the balcony railing exposing her rear end to the world represents a new way of seeing things. She is upside down and her vision is completed reversed. I also think she signifies the courage that it takes to face your shadow. You must be able to show your true self to the world instead of hiding behind a façade. A child always signifies a new way of being.

The symbol of the child was puzzling to me at first, and she was embarrassing. In my old notes I had written something on that dream and I had left that symbol out. I remember not wanting to mention her in recounting the dream those many years ago. However, that was the very thing the dream was saying—you need to look at yourself honestly if you are to grow, even if this means exposing the fact that you are different, odd, and sinful. The expression "a little child shall lead them" speaks of the unquestioning and trusting nature of a child that is required to reach a deeper understanding of God and thus enter into a new life.

That hidden house symbolized my mother's depth and beauty that I had not recognized because I had to separate myself out from her to become who I was meant to be. She had a strong need to be thought of as a good mother because of her own insecurity, and that meant a lot was expected of me; I felt like she was trying to live through me. I had to pull away from her to become an individual. This dream allowed me to see her beauty by showing me the value of her house (herself) and her actual worth. The cream painted exterior represented the façade she presented to the world that hid her natural beauty. I recognized her true value more completely than I ever had prior to this dream.

The scene with the stained glass windows proclaims my Christian heritage (the Trinity). It is interesting to see the contrast between that and the three small plastic windows I first saw and wanted to buy. Those were not a part of me but outside myself (not my heritage). I had discovered my Christianity.

That rocking chair paints a picture of the strength of my ancestry and its importance as the very basis of my being. It was heavy and indestructible yet offered unyielding support. It did not sit rigidly in place but was made for rocking babies and providing comforting rest. The dream told me where I had come from, where I was and where I would be going. I now knew that I would be walking my journey as an individual rather than someone with a cookie-cutter mentality, and I had substance derived from my heritage.

When I look back over this amazing period in my life I realize I found a faith in God that is all encompassing. It brought me an appreciation of my heritage and a realization that not all of life can be measured, touched nor can it be examined by applying the scientific method. It showed me that God is eternal and omniscient, and I have only to be receptive the presence of Spirit. God loves and cares for me; therefore, I don't have to be afraid. And all of this is a gift that was meant for sharing.

The following poem was published in Unity Magazine in the October, 1980 issue.

NEW LIFE

At each approaching death,
and there are many,
I fall into fear again,
dreading each new birth,
each new beginning, bracing, clinging
to the edge of change.
Why so much value
given outworn spaces,
seeking comfort in the familiar?
The pain
is in the crowding.
Life crammed into
restrictive places
and rigid tension
born of fear
block life's flow
and starve the spirit.

We forget to trust,
resist release,
insist on old ways of being,
long outgrown patterns,
once open channels,
now narrow, shallow places.

At last the building tension
burst its bonds,
expelling, thrusting.
Reluctantly I spiral upward,
frightened by the fear of dying,
frightened by the fear of living.

The fresh and spacious
dawning beauty of new life
now greets me.
A sense of joy
and peacefulness
floods through me.
Perhaps at last
I've come of age,
the rights of passage
now completed.
The long succession
of dreams that grew
to wishes, hopes,
and then to trust,
still seemed lacking.
Now I have an inner knowing.
This death has been the birth of faith.

Part 2
The Second Half Of Life

Chapter 10
Enter Eric

Spirit gifted my life when Eric McMaster and I finally found one another. I am tempted to say Eric was my soul mate, but that is such a trite way of putting it. Yet how else does one describe someone who is such a wonderful match? We were born 6 days apart, which meant he could always tease me about being older.

We were born in very different places; he came from Northern Ireland and I was born in Texas. Which leads me into an interesting story. I first heard about him in a reading from a psychic. Before this triggers your disbelief and skepticism, let me say something about psychics. They are people who, for some unexplained reason are very intuitive. When choosing to go to one, always pick one who has a good reputation, and I don't mean someone who advertises with a big, garish sign attached to the front of his or her house. Go to someone you've heard about from some friend.

If you decide to go to a psychic, here are a few words of advice: Don't accept everything they say with an unquestioning manner. Their own thoughts and beliefs may get projected into the reading, or something completely invalid may appear, like, "You're going to Russia, soon." Put that on hold, at least.

The reason I had readings from psychics in those days is that they often gave me an idea about what I might be working on in terms of my life's journey. I was, and am, committed to personal growth. I believe that problems have a way of occurring as challenges from which I can learn, and that is the way the personality unfolds. I believe that Spirit is at work in our lives and we may be too involved in what is happening at the moment to understand the lesson or to see the overview. It is not necessary to go to a psychic; it was merely a choice I made because I felt it might be helpful.

The first reading I ever got was out of curiosity, and I went to Carol Huffstickler, an amazingly psychic who was working in Houston at the time. I came away from that reading in a state of shock because of her accuracy. Carol's readings focused on what you would be dealing with during the following six months, and from that point on I went to her regularly. Several years passed and Carol had moved out of town, so I inquired among friends, found a reputable psychic and made a date for a reading with Silvia Radford.

She was from England and had an accent that I found pleasing. Silvia was very religious and said a prayer at the beginning of the reading. As the reading took place, she would pause while she received information, then she would make her intuitive pronouncement and follow that with the word "Selah" which appears in the Psalms.

She talked about where I was in life, so to speak, and she predicted some things that came true. Some of these things I realized later were related to Eric. I was divorced at the time, feeling sort of left out in terms of relationships and disappointed in myself because I didn't have a partner. However, she said to me, "You think you'll never marry again, but you will. You had things from past lives to finish up, and you took care of that; now someone you know will enter your life in a new way."

Eric was at the end of a marriage that had died several years before, so we were in similar situations. However, I knew him only casually when I went to Silvia, and I never dreamed we had a future together. In my reading, Silvia said to me, "I see you drinking from the same cup with a man, (not from two cups, but one), and there are people gathered around you who seem to be family members.

"I see two fish swimming upstream and they don't come back. Sometimes they do, you know; some marriages don't last, but this one will. He is someone you know, and he is someone who came from farther north." She paused, then said (of all things), "He likes onions."

She may have said more, but that's all I remembered about the person I would marry, and I certainly didn't take that very seriously. Silvia did describe something vaguely about the windows of my house. I had bought a new condo and had chosen blinds that folded horizontally and out of almost transparent material. Those blinds were very unusual, and were selected to let in light yet offer privacy. She described how they appeared when looking out of the condo.

I didn't pay much attention to the reading until Eric and I began dating, then I remembered the things she said. From the start, our time together was filled with joy and meaningful events, and we found we had almost identical religious and philosophical beliefs.

He arrived early on our first date and waited patiently in the living room until I made my appearance. When I stepped into the room, he gasped and said, "You're wearing a tartan!' (I had on a new plaid dress made of dark red voile.)

He came close and gave me a hug while he explained that a tartan was a plaid that identified some particular clan in Scotland. As he began talking about his British background, I listened, but I was also assessing him.

Both he and I were on the Executive Board of the Unity Church of Christianity I had started attending after I had gotten back in touch with my Spiritual beliefs. He was the president and I was a new addition to the Board. We were always seated around a table when we were with one another at meetings. I had always thought of him as handsome and slim, and now I realized he was tall (another plus in my estimate). He was impeccably dressed in suit and tie and at ease with his choice. He worked for the Houston Chronicle Newspaper in National Advertising, and suit and tie were his regular attire. This pleased me; it would be nice to go out with someone who looked well dressed. I also knew he was a person who was admired and was well liked.

Eric suggested we go to a certain restaurant for dinner, and its entire theme was British. I found myself fascinated with him and with the British memorabilia used in the decor. The emphasis on his British background was interesting.

He stressed his family connection to the Scottish people. He gave me a little history lesson about Northern Ireland having voted to be a part of Great Britain while Ireland had voted to become the Irish Free State in 1936.

Later in our relationship I learned he liked onion sandwiches, a combination I had never even imagined. He gave them up when he discovered I thought they would smell horrible.

We fell deeply in love, and we each felt like we'd unexpectedly found a missing puzzle piece we'd been looking for all of our lives.

One of the highlights of our courtship was attending a grand exhibition of "Her Majesty's Royal Marine Band" and "The Argyll and Sutherland Highlanders, Band, Pipes, Drums and Dancers". The music was spectacular, and the precision marching was unbelievable.

The band uniforms were a dark blue and members wore white helmets and carried gleaming silver instruments. The Argyll Highlanders wore kilts and white spats covering their shoes.

The following day, we went again to stand on the periphery of an open lot near Rice Stadium and watch the band march into the lot playing. A little shop that specialized in goods imported from the British Isles had sponsored the band's appearance. As I write of this, chills still run over my body.

The fun part of this event was that after playing some numbers, the band left the lot and marched around Westberry Square, the adjoining shopping district. The people who had been watching hesitated not one minute; they fell in behind the band and marched with it right down the middle of the street. What a motley group it was—young and old, all sorts of dress. If prizes had been awarded, first place would have been given to a mother pushing a baby in a carriage with a couple of floating, red balloons bobbing along above it, and a British flag taped on the hood.

The weather was very hot and humid, and the unfortunate band members were dressed in wool uniforms. We were close enough to smell the damp wool and see the perspiration rolling down their flushed faces. The drum major sported an enormous shako and even its plume looked somewhat wilted, but I'm sure they never played for a more enthusiastic audience.

Later, Eric and I attended a luncheon in a hotel where a small portion of the band played special numbers. They stood in the middle of the room, and I sat inches away from a band member. I can still remember the scent of his damp wool kilt. I loved every minute of that day.

Since both sides of my family, (particularly my father's), included musicians, I felt a sense of identity with the band members. My ancestors must have played instruments in bands similar to this, but I'm sure they never went on tours to foreign countries.

While we dated, we relished going to places that were connected with Great Britain. Our weekend entertainment often included visiting the little store that had sponsored the band. On one occasion, I remarked that my maternal grandmother's name was McMath, and we searched for it on a map of the British Isles that was on display; it showed where different clans had originated. To my surprise, McMath was a sept of the Mathison clan, and it was located—not in Scotland where we had begun looking—but in Northern Ireland. In fact, I later looked at book on the genealogy of my father's family, the Pharrs, and found they came to the States from Ulster–exactly where Eric had come from, and this is an area approximately 150 miles long and 50 miles wide. Five brothers immigrated to the United States from Ulster, Northern Ireland during the 1700s seeking religious and political freedom.

I had never been particularly interested in my ancestors, but now my life took on a deeper dimension. I realized I had roots, and I knew that in some strange way, Ulster was my home too.

During our courtship, poetry continually spilled from my pen, and I am going to include one here as these poems express so much of our joy.

ITS SPRING AGAIN

Reel in the kite,
soaring spirit of my mind –
remember,
there is ground
beneath your feet
and matter to be tended.
The vibrant string
tugs at my hand
inviting me
to spring's rebirthing
as my heart
sings with the wind,
"I am alive,
I am alive again."

And the same energy
that pushes seeds
from dark, earthen wombs
to seek the cobalt sky
in verdant unfolding,
surges through
my April being.
"I am alive.
I am alive, again."

Another instance that demonstrated to me how Spirit worked in our lives occurred when Eric and I went to me see my parents in Corpus Christi before we were married. From the beginning of the visit, both my mother and father were comfortable with him and really liked him. While we were visiting in the living room, something very unusual happened. Eric explained that he had wanted to bring a special edition of the National Geographic magazine with him because it had an article on Northern Ireland in it. One photograph was of a young boy attired for school in a blazer and cap that were like Eric had worn as a student. He hadn't been able to find the copy of the magazine to bring with him.

For some unknown reason I suddenly rose and went to my parent's bedroom, which I seldom entered. I went directly to a wrought iron bookrack where some old copies of National Geographic had been kept for ages. I picked one up and looked at it. It was the very copy Eric wanted to show my parents, and that volume was twenty years old! I returned to the living room in a state of shock firmly believing I was a participant in a miracle.

I had a dream right before I started going with Eric that I remembered later and realized it was precognitive. I had a dream where I was told that I "had run the race and had finished it". I remember discussing it with a psychiatrist friend with whom I had lunch the following day.

Eric was as pleased as I was to find we shared so much in common and appreciated my excitement over discovering my own background. We married less than a year after we started dating. Soon after that, the Chronicle was sold to the Hearst Corporation, and Eric was given a chance to take early retirement. I closed out my practice, and we moved to Fort Clark, an old cavalry fort owned by the private sector. The little town of Brackettville, which had come into existence when the fort was active, sat across the highway, and we soon found common interests doing volunteer work for the Episcopal Church. We both became members of Rotary and I began painting again in the wonderful art studio created from a large building that had housed soldiers in the motor pool when the Fort was active.

We were able to visit his relatives in the British Isles twice while he was still in good health. The first visit was taken not long after we retired. It served to introduce me to the family, and that was a joy. I felt I had known them somewhere in the past, and Northern Ireland felt like home.

When we reached London, his niece and nephew picked us up at Heathrow Airport and took us to their house. We called Northern Ireland and spoke to Eric's older brother. I heard his beautiful, melodious voice say, "Welcome to the McMaster clan. Are you doing bravely?" That was a commonly used phrase in Northern Ireland and it's just a way of saying, "How are you?" I loved being considered a part of the clan.

Our second visit came only a year later, when Eric's brother died unexpectedly. We heard about it on the weekend and decided to go for the funeral. We had to wait until Monday morning to retrieve our passports from the safety deposit box at the local bank before we could leave. Being there for that funeral solidified my membership in that family.

After the funeral and a visit with relatives, Eric and I traveled to Scotland. We went to the Museum at Edinburgh high on a hill that had been part of a fortress years ago. Old band uniforms were displayed in glass cases, and the tailoring on them was flawless. The one that stands out in my memory was a scarlet wool jacket decorated with gold braid. Again, I felt this deep connection to this part of the world and especially with the music and the pageantry.

We just happened to be at the site of the church when a funeral was being held for someone of importance. Many of the men attending were dressed in kilts. We actually saw the end of the ceremony when the lone piper exited the church while playing Amazing Grace. It was absolutely breath-taking.

My love for his family was already formed by the time we went on the second visit, and after we returned home I suddenly sat up in the bed one Sunday morning and a poem poured into my mind. I grabbed a nearby yellow pad and pen and wrote swiftly. It was entitled, "The Funeral," and it later won first place in the category of poems from the community in a contest given by the Southwest Texas Junior College in nearby Uvalde and was published in their 1989 Creative Arts Magazine, "The Palm's Leaf".

I've always felt that the poem was a gift from Spirit that served to validate my own root system; it somehow demonstrated the connection in consciousness between our families. I believe we were connected to one another not only at that present time but linked in our past.

Eric's niece and nephew and their families came to see us later on separate visits, and his nephew returned and represented the family when Eric died a few years later.

THE FUNERAL

We streaked through midnight sky,
arrows piercing time and space,
to be here-to say goodbye
to that waxen shell
that is not you at all.
You've gone.
Your arrow has pierced boundaries
I cannot know,
or perhaps you hover overhead
to watch us gather here.

In a somber room
that pretends to be a home,
a bay window embraces the casket,
now closed,
the cold satin
on which your body lies,
hidden beneath the polished wood.
(not being you at all.)
Words are spoken-
fall unobtrusive as autumn leaves
that mark another season passed.
Now the pallbearers strain
to lift their burden
and step uncertainly
on damp cobblestones.
The funeral director,
decorous in top hat and tails,
leads them to the black
and shining hearse,

its back door gaping open
to swallow casket and flowered wreaths
and shut us out.

I struggle to sort new from old—
the old feeling more real,
more familiar—
like memories recorded in my genes
now unexpectedly exposed
like tree roots
pulled from the earth, suddenly.
The gravesite,
edged by the Irish Sea,
is sheltered by a high rock wall,
assaulted by the chilling wind
and salty spray.
I stand shivering,
my jacket clutched tightly
against my chest,
amidst graves crowded together,
one atop another,
generations layered.
Tall, slender, tilting slabs
that name each site,
were planted long ago
in freshly dug earth
to settle crookedly
as the years passed by.

I am here—a woman—
one of three,
surrounded by the village men,

clad in dark wool suits
and ceremonial black ties.
They watch us with curiosity—
we who have come from afar.
Their women folk
wait for us at home
with freshly brewed hot tea,
in a house filled with scents
of baked scones.
I sit among them
in this alien place
that is not strange at all,
listening to the rhythm,
the lilt of voice
so pleasing to my ear.
We speak of you,
and they recount stories
of the past while
I have only recent memories,
and I wonder if you're here,
if you linger while we speak,
and I feel warm inside.
How strange it is to feel such joy
here with people
I have learned to love.
And I know
if I could dig
to the deeper levels of my own
past generations,
I'd find them
buried there with you.

Chapter 11
Retirement

Fort Clark Springs was a welcomed change from life in the city of Houston. It was an oasis in the desert with huge mulberry trees and a creek that ran close to our townhouse. Our neighbors were friendly people, and we formed a close friendship with some delightful people who came down from Canada to spend the winter months.

My father died a year or so after we moved to Fort Clark, and we moved my mother into a nearby townhouse. Then we persuaded my aunt to join us, and she moved into a townhouse next to my mother's. Later Mother bought and moved into a townhouse that adjoined ours.

As soon as Eric and I settled into our new home, I unconsciously went into my new-person-in-town-mode that I had perfected during my school years when we moved from town to town. This entailed a plan for fitting as seamlessly as possible into the community in hopes of becoming an integral part of it as soon as possible. This would be easy to accomplish with a husband who was handsome, charming and extroverted. We both were eager to meet people and willingly entered into volunteer work that could substitute for careers left behind in retirement.

I had always thought of retirement as the end of all good things and that one would coast down hill to the finish of life. This was anything but what it was actually like. I hit the ground running out of my fear of becoming obsolete, and I was president of several organizations before the end of the year. The residents at Fort Clark knew a good thing when they saw it. They quickly put both Eric and me to work while they played golf, bridge, swam the Fort's Olympic sized pool, or indulged in whatever pleased them along with doing volunteer work.

We soon learned to combine our work with play and found that often the two could not be separated. We learned to play golf and rode the course in our golf cart gleefully singing "Follow the Yellow Brick Road". We had fun and made many friends. We enjoyed just being with one another; even going to the larger border town of Del Rio to go shopping at a larger grocery store was an adventure.

Our interest in meditation was something we didn't talk about since we thought that would not be understood in our new environment, but both of us meditated on a regular basis and shared a somewhat mystical bent that we kept to ourselves.

In retirement I continued to keep my dream journal while Eric, a typical extravert who had brief dreams in contrast to my long, elaborate ones, did not bother to record his. He marveled at the number of pages I wrote in that journal each morning and was fascinated with sharing the meanings I gleaned from mine.

We started attending the Episcopal Church because there was no Unity church in Brackettville, and I had mentioned once being an Episcopalian. One visit to that church and Eric fell in love with it because it was so similar to the Methodist church he had attended in Northern Ireland; he felt right at home.

Some time later, after we had become active, we were scheduled to go with the local minister and his wife to the Church Council meeting in Corpus Christi. The night before we were to leave I had a significant dream. I saw a chalice with oil in it sitting on the sidewalk going into the Parish Hall. I hadn't even thought about it and certainly hadn't analyzed it, when we left to drive to Corpus. For some reason it popped into my mind and I related it. The minister's wife said, "Healing! Oil is a symbol of healing." And so it was. The sidewalk was a pathway leading into the place where the congregation gathered to share meals, a typical part of church life. That church and the people in it did become an important part of our life. Personally I felt it served to heal my attitude about myself because I still carried the guilt of past failures at marriage.

It is interesting to me that we later went to a Cursillo, which is an intensely spiritual weekend sponsored by the Episcopal Church. We went to one named "The Cursillo of the Forgiving Heart". That weekend was very meaningful to both of us, and we served as team members that presented Cursillos in the years to come.

Rev. John Dunham was the priest at our Cursillo, and the entire group has met in reunion once a year since that time. The members have remained close despite living in different places, and as I presently write we have had twenty-one annual reunions.

Our church activity was our primary interest, but we both also became members of Rotary and attended weekly meetings. It was an active group doing service work in the community, and the programs were so interesting that I began writing them up for the local newspaper. This practice seemed to take on a life of its own. The articles grew larger and larger. Soon they were published on the front page each week. This continued until I began having hearing problems that made it too difficult for me to report accurately. The newspaper staff protested that they sorely missed my "column," and even some readers complained.

***

One extraordinary thing happened when we had been living at the Fort for a few years. We would drive into San Antonio for doctor's appointments every now and then. We went to the excellent local clinic in Brackettville for small matters, however when we felt a need to consult specialists, we preferred going to the Medical Center in San Antonio. We would usually stop at Castroville to have dinner at a motel that was perched on a hilltop overlooking the town, spend the night and make a special occasion out of the trip. I'll always remember one of them.

It was our custom to arrive early in San Antonio and spend our waiting time in a bookstore near the Medical Center. On one trip I walked into that store, and at the entry sat a table loaded with books for sale at reduced prices; I stopped to browse and immediately picked up a book. I wasn't attracted by it's black and white cover, but had noticed its title: "The Mier Expedition Diary: A Texan Prisoner's Account by Joseph D. McCutchan", Edited by Joseph Milton Nance.

That book had "jumped out at me" and I opened it to the very page that recounted my own maternal great grandfather's role in this historical event. He was several generations removed, but he was my ancestor.

"It would be an act of palpable and base injustice to close this chapter and not bid adieu to the incidents of the battle without mentioning with praise the name of Doctor Wm. F. McMath, who, though perhaps he fired not a gun—or at any rate very few shots, performed other services of a more valuable nature which could not have been dispensed with. There were other Doctors present, but they would pay no attention to the wounded. McMath was without surgical experience, or even practical experience as a physician, but he had read and knew something of the treatment due to broken limbs; and though he was anxious to make his rifle speak "volumes" to the enemy, yet he saw men suffering around him, possessed with genuine feelings of bravery and humanity, he smothered and conquered the feelings of ambition, set aside his rifle, and took up the hemp and splinters. He was often as much exposed as those who were engaged with the enemy; but over-attentive to the humane duty devolving upon him as a human being, he relieved the pains of the dying, calmed the tormenting pangs of those who suffered with broken limbs, however exposed might be his situation, without one sign of dread or fear. If any man deserves the blessing of those poor wounded fellows, it is Doctor McMath; if any service performed upon that day is more worthy of remembrance than another, that of McMath merits the preeminence; if there was a duty performed worth of the truly brave man, and the Christian, that duty was performed by McMath; and if there is one man who, for his deeds upon that memorable day, merits the praise of the Brave, the generous and the good throughout the world, that man is Doctor Wm. F. McMath. His reward will be greater than man can bestow; and though the accounts of that Expedition call Doctor Sinixon the surgeon of the army, who never performed one of the duties of a surgeon, McMath enjoys the pleasing consciousness of having done his duty as such – of having administered to the comfort of his suffering fellow creatures when no one else would take that trouble, and may he long live to enjoy that reflection and finally meet the reward of the truly brave, the good and the Christian in a world eternal and beyond the grave."

The Expedition occurred in 1844–46. McMath was a member of the group that was later captured by Mexicans and was marched toward Mexico City. At some point, they stopped. Each man was blindfolded and made to draw a bean from a jar containing both black and white beans. Those who drew a black one were shot on the spot. McMath luckily drew a white one. He actually wrote a letter to his family while listening to the shots of those being killed. My family had the original letter, but it was somehow was lost decades ago.

This book had "jumped out at me" and I opened it to the very page that recounted my great grandfather's role in this historical event. Finding that book and learning of his significant participation in the incident was clearly a gift from Spirit. Of course, I bought the book immediately.

After that, the realization that I had such a fine man as an ancestor brought me a great sense of validation as I cherished the thought of having his genes within my own being. Once again I had been shown the importance of my genetic heritage, and I was reassured that synchronistic events had not been left behind me in Houston.

Of course I told people about this occurrence; it was too astounding to keep to myself, but I did not often speak openly about the unusual experiences of the past that had helped validate my Spiritual beliefs. However, I'm sure that I told those who had become my close friends about that book. There were several aspects of my life that I did not feel free to discuss. As long as I had lived in the anonymity of the city, this had not seemed important. When I retired to a small town, however, I wanted to be seen being like other people—not different. I avoided speaking of the fact that both Eric and I had been divorced, but they did know that we were practically still on our honeymoon. However, I had put away some of the very things that had played an important role in my life.

I even felt uncomfortable sharing the fact that I had been a mental health professional. I had learned from past experiences that mental health professionals had a potential for evoking fear of exposure. People in small towns, as well as some city folk, tend to suspect that therapists indulge in instant diagnosis—one look and the emperor would be exposed as wearing no clothes. Put more simply, some of them seemed to be afraid I'd see them as crazy. This may sound ridiculous but it's true, and this served to diminish my very personality—like I had disowned a part of my own personhood, but I didn't realize that until a long time later.

I guess there are therapists who view the world through such skewed lenses, but I was certainly not one of them. To be safe, however, I tucked away references to my past career and deleted any jargon that reeked of psychology— no "shrink-speak" came from me. It wasn't a complete denial of my background though, because I did want to be respected for my accomplishments.

Actually, therapists are the last persons to think of any kind of behavior as being strange because we've seen it all and know everyone is a little bit crazy. Most of us therapists have examined our own foibles relentlessly in order to be clear in our assessments and interaction with clients. Any therapist caught in denial by his peers would be laughed at and judged as having chosen the wrong profession. Generally speaking, any therapist worth his salt is open and non-defensive, and this makes them prone to occasionally shock non-professionals with their frankness.

The Fort had a wonderful art studio that had been converted from an old barrack. A spacious central room accommodated tables and easels where beds had once stood. We were on the second floor, natural light poured in through a series of large windows. Two baths and a small kitchen area provided plenty of sinks for the cleanup so necessary for people using paint. Two smaller rooms were useful; in one supplies were kept on hand for members, and the other housed frames. The studio was within walking distance of our townhouse.

I eagerly took my easel and box of oil paints to the studio and selected an empty table as my own little area. Again, my alarm bells went off. My easel was heavy and well constructed, contrasting with the lightweight, unsteady ones provided by the Art Club. My paint box was a wooden one made by Winton (then the top of the line for Art paraphernalia) and therefore was the sign of a serious painter. Oops! I'd better watch out–better tone it down.

When I first saw the studio I thought that I would be a perfect place to express my artist-self without reservation, but I found myself tending to paint what I thought would be liked and what might sell rather than expressing myself freely. I didn't realize, it, but I was again not letting my creative energy flow unimpeded.

During the first years that I lived in Fort Clark the Art group members consisted mostly of retirees who were learning to paint for the first time. They quickly regarded me as an old-timer who could offer them an opportunity to learn from someone with experience. An audience of viewers stood behind me and watched my every stroke when I began my first painting. At the end of the day and I wanted to clean up and go home, I felt like I should put a sign on the easel that said, "This is not finished; it's just a first coat." My desire to be perfect also emerged and took charge. As the days went on I unconsciously started trying to paint a finished picture rather than build it up with coat after coat. If the canvas was too large for that, I would paint one little portion in a finished way instead of developing the whole canvas in incomplete, general areas that would show whether the composition was good.

As the years went on the members attended many workshops and painted so much that they became quite competent, and some went on to win numerous rewards in shows in that area. For a while I took an active role in the Art community. I gave some workshops and taught Art to some children. I joined the Art League in Del Rio and won first prize of a group portrait of my father's family orchestra. I was proud of that accomplishment, but I knew that copying a photograph as I had done was not truly creative.

Over time I painted less and less. One factor was that I needed silence and tended to psychologically disappear into my creative thoughts when painting. Being around fellow painters and friends made it tempting to visit and talk rather than to paint, and I slowly stopped doing much painting. The muse became disenchanted and withdrew to resurface again through writing.

My writer-self jumped back into activity when I happened to visit the amphitheater at Fort Clark and looked at the stage; I had a flash. "Wow! What a great place to find a body." I thought and then a title popped into my head– "Death Plays the Lead". Since I was not inclined to be a murderer, I directed my creative energy into writing a mystery. (Only a mystery buff and a dedicated writer would have had that kind of reaction). Trusting my intuition, I never considered changing that title; I knew it was a gift from Spirit.

I had attended a writing group in Houston for years and now I was continuing writing after retirement. I had already written a couple of mysteries I hadn't even tried to get published. I began slaving away at writing this mystery and when it was finished, I sent it to Houston to be critiqued by my dear friend, Guida Jackson, who was in that writer's group and had around twenty books of her own published by that time. Some time later after she had read it, she called and said, "I'm starting a publishing company and I want to publish your book."

To say that I was startled doesn't do it justice; Eric had to peel me off the ceiling. I couldn't imagine having such good fortune and of course joyously agreed. I decided the book was too short and added a subplot that fitted miraculously in and added to the intricacy of the plot. As soon as I finished it I sent it to her and the publishing process began.

Before it came off the press, however, something turned my life upside down. Eric and I had gone to San Antonio for check-ups with our physicians. We had appointments at the same time with different doctors. When I was through, I waited for him to join me, but he didn't arrive. I finally received a phone call that told me to meet him at his doctor's office. When I got there, he was sitting there attached to a machine that was recording his heart's activity. Jagged, erratic lines reflected on the screen screamed trouble ahead!

He wasn't allowed to go home; I dashed back to the Fort, stuffed clothes into a suitcase, and scurried back prepared to stay indefinitely. He went into Methodist Hospital and had a six-way bypass and a valve repair. He was on the operating table all day long. Friends of mine had arrived from Brackettville to stay with me during the surgery as well as Episcopalian friends we knew in San Antonio, however, all but one had returned home as the time dragged into night. My good friend Wendy Lampkin was still there where a nurse called from the operating room around 9:00 p.m. to tell me it "looked grim". Wendy and I stood up and put our arms around each and started to pray. Another lone woman in the waiting room asked if she could join us. The three of us prayed for God's will to be done, but we would like for him to live.

As we finished, the nurse called back and said, "We were busy getting the life support machine ready, and we turned around to discover that he had finally stabilized. We didn't have to hook him up to it." Our prayers had been answered. With great relief and thankfulness, Wendy left to drive home to Brackettville and go to work the next morning while I went to stay with a friend. However, I was awakened at 4:00 A.M. to be told he had started bleeding again and that they had to go back in and take care of that, but he clung to life.

We had been very active in the Episcopal Church and had gotten to know many people in the West Texas Diocese, and the love and support we received during his hospital stay and the years he had left was amazing. The same was true of Brackettville; I learned later that the next Sunday after his operation, every church in Brackettville prayed for his recovery.

I moved to San Antonio and stayed there during the time Eric was hospitalized. I didn't even go home when it turned cold, but went out and bought a coat. One day I went into ICU to find him not making good sense, and it was very frightening even though I knew the isolation and the surroundings encouraged this kind of disorientation. When I left, I went to the waiting room and sat where I could watch the hall in case one of his doctors might walk by. It wasn't a doctor who came, however, it was a priest.

That day Father John Dunham happened to come see us, and he approached me walking down that hall with the Communion elements in his hands, and we went directly into ICU. We had communion at Eric's bed standing directly at each side of him. John laughed and said, "I'll bet they think we are administering last rites."

He explained afterwards that he had been driving somewhere in Llano, where he was pastor of that church, and got the feeling that we needed him, and he simply came. The intuitive message he received was Spirit at work. My prayer for help had been answered.

I guess no one realizes the magnitude of God's presence until they come face to face with death. Several times during those months I felt the presence of Spirit and saw Christ in the face of other caring people.

Eric hovered near death for a very long time. The surgery was September the eleventh, and we returned home the day before Thanksgiving. We had no more than entered the gates of Fort Clark before we saw a big sign saying, "Welcome Home Eric" with signatures of friends all over it. How wonderful that was!

For the next few precious years, he was able to be active in a limited way by dragging along a portable oxygen tank that we called Fido. We "walked Fido"; I even made it a nametag that looked like a license plate hung around the handle, and we decorated it for Christmas. We even got to attend a Cursillo reunion, and when the group started to walk up a small, hill to hold services in the Chapel some of the men picked up Fido and tenderly carried him up the hill so that Eric could be with us.

A glass wall stood behind the altar at the Chapel where we held the reunions, and directly beyond that was a large bronze statue of Christ with arms outstretched. In was in this space that Eric's ashes were scattered in a reunion service following his death.

We had squeezed the best out of each moment he had left after his operation, and I had a lot of adjusting to do when he was finally gone. He died in October and my book was published that coming spring. It was dedicated to Eric, and it served me well by keeping me occupied with marketing.

The love and support I experienced, as well as the prayers that were answered during Eric's illness, were an expression of the energy of God that is hard to define or describe, but I came to know it well. I had come to believe that God constantly expresses in our everyday lives through Spirit.

It took me six years after Eric's death before I was ready to make the move. I needed to leave Fort Clark because I needed to closer to family, but it was hard to leave my friends, and my son's work entailed traveling and he was seldom home.

At that time, he was working as a sound tech doing sound for such things as television magazine shows. This is fascinating work that takes him where news is breaking, but this means being at home in small increments of time. He finally decided to make a career change so that he would have more time at home; however he still does some sound work. The thing that finally inspired me to move was that he built a house, and I moved to Wimberley to be closer to him and his two adult children.

My daughter, Sharon, had suggested that I move to San Diego where she lives and works as a massage therapist and an artist. She and a friend frequently give workshops designed to help women get in touch with their own strength and wisdom through accessing their own inner connection with Spirit. California was certainly a possibility, but it would never seem like home to me, and I chose Wimberley.

I had visited my son many times and had been with him when he chose to buy the land on which he built his home. When Sharon and India had visited from California, we walked the site and had fantasized about where my house would be placed. The next time I visited Doc his house was under construction and we knew I would soon take the leap and join him. He had just returned from Iraq having done sound for the Sixty Minutes TV program with Scott Pelley showing viewers Sadam Hussein's "spider hole retreat".

A few months later I suddenly had a chance to rent the townhouse in which I lived on the Fort to an ideal prospective renter; the only catch was that she needed to move within a week. At this point in time I had to deal with my own things plus the household goods and property that I had inherited from my mother and my aunt when they had passed on. I got rid of as many of the excess household items that I could, kept what would be needed to rent the places furnished, and temporarily stored the remainder in order to vacate my townhouse.

It took two warehouse units to hold my accumulated possessions. If I were a person who found organization simple, it would not have been such a daunting task, but it was unbelievably difficult, and I soon lost track of what was where to a large extent. All of this was finally accomplished in a week!

The blessing that made it all possible was my wonderful friend, Anna Renken. She had once rented the townhouse adjoining mine and we had formed a deep friendship. Later, she purchased a large home and moved, and when I needed to vacate my townhouse, I was able to move in with her and stayed there for three months. She was also invaluable help during the actual move.

My neighbors and friends were aghast at the thought of me leaving, and I learned later that many thought it a mistake, but it wasn't. They wondered how I could leave such a loving environment. I knew this was a valid concern, but I wanted to make the move when I was still able to do the work myself rather than being a burden on my children. My house was ready in Wimberley, and I was waiting for the connections to be made before actually moving there when St. Andrew's members gave me a farewell party. I thought it would just be a getting together of communicants and friends from my old neighborhood who would bring a dish to eat together at Anna's house, but it turned out to be an extravaganza.

The Church service was dedicated to me in honor of 20 years of service I had given. (How could it have been that long?) Anna had invited the entire congregation for a farewell party after church, and as soon as we got to her house, people began arriving with all sorts of food. We had a wonderful meal and after that Rev. Nathan Lafrenz, the Lutheran minister who also served the Episcopalians, presided over a ceremony where they presented me with a certificate for those years of service, and I was given a beautiful gold cross and chain.

I thanked them from the bottom of my heart and spoke of the years I had spent in the church. I had moved around most of my early life and the fact that I had actually been there 20 years surprised me. I recounted that the first time we went to church at St. Andrew's only four or five people were there, and it was dark because they couldn't afford to turn on the lights while running the air conditioner. A supply priest had come from Del Rio to do the service. Some time later the Bishop was coming for a visit and Eric and I , who were now active members, showed up to help clean the church and Parish Hall. Only three ladies were there, and all were far older than we and one was legally blind! I ended my talk by saying that in those early days Eric and I had been joined by my mother and aunt and we all attended church together, but the congregation had been very small. Now we had a much larger congregation, and I was the only one of my family left. It was now time for me to go.

The back porch of Anna's house proved to be a natural stage as the yard sloped down then leveled off, allowing people to sit in chairs and be an audience. Several accomplished musicians played their instruments and sang. Everyone loved the music and we enjoyed ourselves immensely. I told someone it was like attending one's own funeral, hearing the kudos yet also getting to eat! What a wonderful thing to have happen.

This was a happy occasion, but there was a certain amount of sadness. Not only was I leaving dear friends and a place that held some wonderful memories, but I was having to face the fact that this move would inevitably be a step toward the end of my own life. Farewells are never easy, but by November I would be in Wimberley living in my new home. We close one door and another opens; a wonderful new adventure lay ahead.

I must tell you that Anna Renken and Rev. Nathan Lafrenz later married and began their own new life adventure to the joy of all who know and love them.

FALL

Summer slipped away
as fall came forth.
Now leaves dying
soon will release
their grip on life.
Some in fear of non-being,
will cling to branches
no longer sustaining,
reluctant to take
the leap of faith,
unable to envision
life transforming,
or imagine
a different way of being.

Chapter 12
Returning Home

"Returning home" seems like a strange choice for this chapter title; but I am now writing about moving to Wimberley to be near my son, and this little town is quite near Austin where I was born and lived during the early years of my life. It feels like home to me.

Building a house in Wimberley would have been impossible since Doc could not possibly oversee the project. I opted on bringing in a modular home. He had worked in construction when he was younger, and so he was able to change the floor plans where needed; we chose larger windows, enlarged the front porch and added height to the pitch of the roof. A few months later the building was brought onto the property and nestled into the beautiful live-oak trees in a way that appeared they had grown up around it. The interior was beautifully done and I found it perfect for my needs and desires.

I performed the task I had done so many times, particularly in my early life—I hung the profusion of oil paintings painted by myself, my mother, my grandmother, and my daughter. Once they were on the wall, it was officially home. We both had what we wanted—we retained our privacy yet were nearby.

Wimberley is an arty community and it quickly felt like I belonged here. I had thought that I would be active in the Art community and might possibly go back to the Unity Church that I had lost access to when we moved to Brackettville despite my ties to the Episcopal church. Nothing like this happened. I found myself again writing rather that painting and after visiting St. Stephen's Episcopal Church and being greeted with such enthusiasm, I never even visited anywhere else. I also knew that St. Stephen's had a very active group of senior citizens and that helped me make the choice.

My son had lived in Wimberley for more than twenty years, and the local people accepted me readily; they didn't see me as an intruder. I soon found myself surrounded with friends and became deeply involved in St. Stephens. The Wimberley community has been a loving and an interesting environment. To top it all off, I was welcomed into a Jung study group that had been meeting for over fifteen years. I was absolutely joyous when I was able to join it.

The Jung group met at Mary Anne McGee's home and the moment I walked into her house and saw a bookcase that covered one whole wall stuffed with books, I felt at home. Mary Anne became my special confidante, and the women who gathered there each week my treasured friends.

I had already adjusted to becoming "older", (I use that term because it doesn't sound as demeaning as saying I had gotten old.) Not only was my own body going south and my hearing questionable, but also friends I had known for years were dying off.

I got up one morning and took a look at the mirror. The following poem came to me, and since I don't allow myself to focus on my old age a lot, I will tuck it in here and move on. It seems to belong here:

MIRROR IN THE MORNING

I saw her in the mirror
as I took my pills—
the ones to support
my aging life.
Are those ears growing larger?
Cover them with hair—
cut short now
where once it hung
in soft, seductive waves
inviting his fingers
to sort it out—
something he didn't have
would call him to me.
I see a hint of breast
beneath my gown—
I remember them
as round and firm,
proudly pointing
at the world in praise of femininity,
knowing their siren's call
would never fail.
He's only a memory now
who visits in the night,
occasionally.
We playfully reach out
for an absent presence
that has left its scent
to bring us pleasure.
I look again at those ears.
I will plug in my hearing aids

and hang incongruously
gay earrings
on these sagging lobes
hoping to draw attention away
and hint at a nonexistent beauty.

I no longer grieve that lost self.
There is a richer Self inside.

When I moved to Wimberley I was exhausted from the move and even the walk from my house to Doc's was tiring. I was feeling my age, but I began to rejuvenate. I soon forgot about, (at least to a great extent) how old I was and how much I had lost in life. Each day I welcomed interesting activities and regained a lot of strengths I thought had disappeared. I was too busy doing fascinating things to worry about my age.

I can't give Wimberley all the credit; part of this was due to having adopted a rescue dog who became my constant and loving companion. I now had a loving family close by, and a four-legged, waggily-tailed critter that greeted me enthusiastically every morning and walked me twice a day despite rain, cold or heat. I found that exercise is good for the brain as well the body, and having an adoring fuzzy-friend who is constantly present and who never misbehaves because she is so grateful at having a good home is a priceless gift.

Anna Renken had called to tell me about a badly treated dog that needed a home. I set aside my misgivings and agreed to take her. My last dog, Heidi, a miniature schnauzer, had died when I was staying with Anna of Rocky Mountain spotted tick fever I had not been able to get diagnosed. Her death had left a space in my heart that needed filling.

The night before Anna brought the rescue dog to me I was thinking about her and wondering how she could be as sweet as Anna had described after having had such a hard life. The dog had been chained to a tree the entire three years of her life and had lost part of the sight in her left eye probably from being hit or kicked.

The word "grace" popped into my mind and refused to leave, so I named her Gracie.

She arrived with all her fur shorn because of mats and tangles; she looked like a large rat with a long, barren tail that bothered me since I was accustomed to poodles and schnauzers with cropped tails. She weighed 15 pounds when she arrived; she now weighs twenty-two. Her fur grew out to be thick and beautiful—she transformed into a bear. She has a variety of colors as if her Maker couldn't quite make up His mind—black, burnt sienna, even a little white. Her tail now wags like a cheerleader's pompom as she joyfully walks with me each day. Gracie is another gift from Spirit.

Some time after Gracie entered my life something else wonderful happened; our Wimberley family went to California on a visit. This trip was very special for me. My wonderful daughter had arranged to hold a "croning ceremony" for me. The word "crone" means an ugly old hag, perhaps even a witch to most people in this society, but in other cultures a crone means a wise, older woman.

A woman's life can be thought of as occurring in three stages. She is maiden, mother, then matron. The meaning of this last stage has been recognized and honored in many cultures. Our own society often discounts and overlooks older woman. In doing so, the value of the wisdom gleaned from many years of life experience is lost or discounted. This also can result in older women losing their feeling of being worthwhile and valued, and this can lead them to give up on life and slide downhill to their passing.

That is changing; since women's lib came in and women entered the market place and assumed less traditional roles, their place in society and their self-concept has changed. Women who cross over into this phase of life move into uncharted territory. There is little room for them in a youth-worshipping, patriarchal culture, but they are creating a new way of being. Since they have found themselves invisible in their world, they have realized their importance to each other and have recognized and valued their own wisdom. Many have spent a good portion of their life serving others; now they have the time and opportunity to pursue and enjoy their own interests. They are finding themselves; they are keeping fit and active in order to attain a healthy longevity.

Sharon has a friend, Anna Carter, who is a psychic, and the two of them give workshops occasionally on personal growth through inner awareness. These are often attended by a group of women who come together to care for and support one another. When I visited, they gathered to perform a croning ceremony for me, and that was meaningful beyond words.

In case you are picturing these women as a bunch of weirdoes, let me tell you that Anna graduated from Rice University with a degree in philosophy, and the group consists of very interesting, competent women, one of whom is actually a nun.

On this visit to California, I was the center of attention and was treated like a queen for that occasion. They dressed me in a colorful robe that even covered my head, and I lay on a mat meditating while Sharon and Anna performed a ceremony. When it ended, the women were circled around me, intently focused and waiting to hear what I had experienced in meditation. Looking at those eager faces I thought I was going to disappoint them; I had expected some earth-shaking image to appear, and I explained that hadn't occurred. I said, "I only saw a woman in a tiered dress of gray chiffon dancing and dancing. I kept trying to make her go away so that something important could happen, but she refused. She just kept dancing!" My audience laughed. That dancing woman was the essence of "cronedom"; I had never seen her face because it was also covered with chiffon. How interesting; this portrayed the invisibility of being an older woman. When you are old, you are finally freed from all the expectations that have been laid upon you. No one, particularly men, even seem to see you. This means you are at last free to dance and any way you please.

As I write this, my Jung study group is starting a new book written by internationally known Japanese-American Jungian psychiatrist Jean Shinoda Bolen, "Goddesses in Older Women, Archetypes in Women Over Fifty", farther down on the cover is the phrase, "Becoming a Juicy Crone". That's what I am—a juicy crone and I love it! Whee!

I returned to Wimberley and resumed my everyday existence, having given up my queendom of that day, but I did feel differently about where I was in life and my self-assurance continued to grow as time passed.

***

The next opportunity to grow came when I enrolled in a four-year course called Education for Ministry, (EFM). It is a study of the Bible from the viewpoint of its historical setting and what research tells us about the possible authors of various books. My short-term memory was not the greatest at this point, and I was afraid that I would not be able to study well enough to handle it. I crossed my fingers and took a leap of faith. Actually, the extensive reading and studying required helped me to become more alert and to realize I could still learn.

The fact that I chose to take this course was in a way unusual. I have never been one to read the Bible studiously. I was turned off by the violence and was aware of the contradictory incidences. I had respect for it but viewed it more as tool to promote a religion that was structured by human beings to serve their own desires for power. During my lifetime I had seen it too often used as an instrument to "prove" arguments and to "prove" certain behavior was right or wrong. However, I had also come to see that using it in that manner was idolatry, and this freed me to study it seriously and in a less prejudiced way.

I attended a get-acquainted meeting and received the text for the first year—a huge notebook filled with reading assignments. The following week the first class was scheduled. I fearfully gathered that unwieldy book in hand and had started out the door to leave for the meeting when a question popped up in my mind. Did I remember the address of where we would meet? My memory was not to be trusted; I'd better check. I went to my office and pulled up the message with directions on the computer and found that I had remembered it correctly. I shut down the computer and was on my way to the car when I realized that I had left my keys on the desk. I turned to go back and realized I had just locked myself out of the house and had no car keys! Horrors!

An extra key was on the porch, but my son had placed it on the doorframe ledge above the door. Neither of us had snapped to the fact that I couldn't reach that high. How could I get it down? I decided to find a stick in the yard and try to knock it down. That was risky because in doing so it could fall through the narrow cracks between the floorboards of the porch. It was my only chance though, and I started for the yard. Suddenly, to my amazement I looked up to see my son striding toward me with a big grin on his face! He had a key that opened my door; I retrieved my own set, left and arrived at the meeting on time.

A small gravel road leads into the property. He ordinarily drives past my home as he goes to his and seldom stops. Why he had turned in that evening, neither of us will ever know, but it was an integral part of that small miraculous occurrence.

The next day I remembered two other happenings that had preceded the key incident. Earlier that morning I had remembered that one of my hearing aids had been sent off for repair and was due back in two weeks. I realized that it should be arriving soon. For some reason, I went to the front door and opened it. A box containing the repaired hearing aid had been delivered and left directly in front of the door on the porch! I would have the advantage of being able to hear better that evening.

Later that same afternoon I had noticed a UPS truck driving up our little road. It had gone past the house and to the end of the road; it was turning around to leave. Neither my son nor I had numbers on the houses because we have post office boxes for our mail; I was worried that the deliveryman had given up, not been able to find my house, and was leaving. I ran for the front door and started for the yard to flag him down. He had already pulled into my driveway, parked and was bringing in the package I had been expecting!

When I meditated on these three surprising instances, I asked, "What are these things telling me?" The answer came to me that I had been living in self-doubt and fear. The message was simply, "Don't be afraid, it will work out. You are not lost. You'll be okay."

That sounds familiar!

***

The following Spring I attended the twentieth yearly reunion my Cursillo group. One of the talks that were presented was on synchronicity. During the discussion period that followed, I related these incidences as illustrations of synchronicity and someone said, "God sure wanted Frances to go to EFM." That's the way I see it too. God acts in our life all the time, sometimes in extraordinary ways.

An interesting event occurred a year or so ago when someone from my past reentered my life in a wonderful way.

If each blue pebble represents a significant event that occurred in my life, this pebble would be one of great value to me, and strangely enough, I hadn't thought to include it in recounting my stories until something happened to jog my memory. I was sitting in church at St. Stephen's one Sunday when I noticed that among the activities listed for the following week was one that said Bishop Dena Harrison would be speaking at the Wednesday night "Halftime" service. I gasped. I knew her. She had played a brief role in my life long ago—and here she was—a Bishop! A female Bishop made it even stranger; not many female bishops exist.

The story begins in Houston where I was in practice. I was asked to give the kick-off speech in a series of programs about mother-daughter relationships at a local Episcopal Church. A book on this subject had recently been published and had quickly shot to the top of the best-seller list. The subject was evidently a compelling one. Before the first program the Houston Chronicle devoted a full page to interviews with the various speakers.

I hadn't snapped to the fact that this meant we would have a large crowd when I left that night to go speak. I didn't take anything written beyond a few scrappy notes since I had never needed anything but a few key words to speak on a subject I knew that well. However, when I drew near I saw cars pouring in from all directions approaching the church. Panicsville! I found a place to park and entered a building teeming with people. I pushed past them on the crowded stairway leading to the room in which I was to speak. I felt absolutely stunned. My God! What was I being called to do? I felt completely unprepared.

So many people had come that they had to move the meeting to the Church proper, and it filled up quickly. I had begun praying the minute I saw the gathering crowd. When I was seated in the sanctuary, which was elevated like a stage, I visualized my ego and addressed her. I imagined putting tape on her mouth and leading her to a chair. I sat her down and said in effect, "This is not your job. Sit down and shut up. You're so frightened you would screw this up for sure." Then I said to the Lord, "Speak through me because I'm in over my head. I am incapable of giving these people what they need;

it's up to you." Simple words scraped into bare essentials aimed at the target like bullets. They hit their mark.

I never missed a beat-never said "Uh". I drew on material gleaned from my Jungian studies. I have no idea who first composed the questions I asked, but they proved to be priceless. "What do you love the most about your mother?" I explained to the listeners that this would be your persona, the face you present to the world. Then I asked, "What do you hate the most about your mother?" I explained this would be your shadow, the part of you that lies outside your awareness.

These questions cut through the top layer of their thoughts and attitudes and began the process of pulling apart the tangle of opposites. This separated out and clarified feelings and gave them permission to own the negative stuff in order to deal with it instead of pushing it into the dark recesses of their unconscious mind where it would continue to furtively sabotage their relationship. It helped them recognize that life doesn't consist of pure-white anything. The grays and the black exist. Feelings simply are; what you do with those feelings is important.

I certainly didn't forget to thank God for taking over and making that speech. The program was an unqualified success, and I later learned that the attendance at the rest of the presentations remained high.

Dena Harrison was one of the two women who had arranged that series of programs, and she had impressed me as a calm, intelligent and exceptionally competent woman. A month or so later I received a call from her. She knew I worked with dreams from a Christian point of view because I had given workshops on this subject, and she had a dream she wanted to discuss with me. She felt the dream was calling her to become a priest. I listened to that dream and went with my intuition. I simply agreed with her. My experience with revelatory dreams had left me with a certainty beyond question that some dreams are messages from Spirit.

I was involved in her life changing decision to enter the priesthood. Much later I was invited to her ordination. You must realize that this was a time when women were just beginning to be accepted into the priesthood, and her accomplishment was no small feat. She had later become the first woman bishop in the Diocese of Texas

I was unable to attend her ordination, however I heard of her over the following years and was proud to know that I had played a role in her becoming a priest. Imagine my feelings when I read that Bishop Dena Harrison was going to be coming to St. Stephens. Bishop! She had become a bishop!

I had seen her at a distance when attending a Women's Gathering at Camp Capers when she was a priest, but I had avoiding meeting her. I had again divorced and remarried. Having done this, I felt like a horrible sinner, and it was something that embarrassed me greatly. When I had seen Dena at the Gathering, I was busy being the perfect wife and partner to my husband, Eric. I knew I had at last done the right thing, but I doubted that anyone else could possibly believe that.

I was holding fast to the image of a stable couple that we had presented in Brackettville and truly were. I was denying the grays and blacks of life and clinging to a non-existent white. I had hidden what I felt was my disjointed, dysfunctional past. I had neither accepted who I was nor come to terms with the reason for my speckled past.

I simply did not feel worthy of speaking to her. I was judging myself by standards that hadn't fit me and yet I felt would have killed my soul if I had not disobeyed them.

I had gotten stuck in the guilt by not wanting to own it. If I had asked for forgiveness, the process of reconciliation could have taken place, but I didn't and I doomed myself to dragging that burden around with me for a very long time.

Besides that–who I am or have been is to be judged only by my Creator, the sin was in my playing god and being unforgiving of myself, and I am ill equipped for that.

It may be difficult to understand the process, but Spirit relentlessly pushes us toward wholeness. We should strive for excellence but recognize that we will never be perfect. I knew for sure that I wasn't perfect—thank goodness! What a bore I'd be if I had gotten what I wanted.

After Bishop Harrison spoke at our church I was able to visit with her. I had wondered if she would remember me, but she recognized me quickly and we had a delightful short visit since other people were waiting for a chance to speak to her. However, seeing her again brought closure to an occurrence in my life that had a lot of meaning and reinforced my feelings that I had returned home.

***

My next avenue of service at St. Stephens came when I joined the Community of Hope and was trained to do such things as providing care for those in need. My assignments consisted of visiting with people who were living at Deer Creek Nursing Home in Wimberley.

Members of Community of Hope meet in small groups once a month to discuss how things are going with their assignments and to give each other a chance to speak of anything that is bothering them and receive support from the group when the work is tough.

At one of the meetings, I was responsible for leading the group through Lectio Divina, which is a way to meditate on a chosen bit of scripture. I had been very pressed for time and did not prepare ahead of time, and I had to explain the process because the other group members had not previously taken part in it. I did Lectio Divina and meditated regularly so I hadn't given it much thought, and I made some mistakes during the exercise. What occurred left an opening in the structure of the presentation for Spirit to enter.

I had inadvertently started what happened by speaking of a terminal patient that was difficult for me to visit for various reasons. Then one woman in our group spoke of how difficult it was for her to undergo chemotherapy for her leukemia, and this opened the way for a man to speak his problem with his Alzheimer's disease, which was growing worse each day. We were sharing one another's concern at a deep level and the feeling tone of that session became magically healing. It was certainly one of those rare occasions when people bared their souls and found solace. I knew my mistake had opened up this opportunity for closeness and that this was the work of Spirit.

***

Shortly after joining St. Stephens, I had wonderful new opportunity to serve. I was asked to join a small group of writers to share the task of writing meditations on scripture that would be sent out to the congregation of St. Stephens by email. This was a task that would replace similar writings formerly done by Father Gahan. The church was growing and he had so much to do that this would be of help to him. Each of us was to write one for each day of an assigned week.

I was reluctant to be included in this group. I saw each of the persons called as much brighter, better informed, and certainly more familiar with the Bible than I was. I did however have faith in my ability to discover basic truths through meditation. At the first meeting of this group I spoke of my misgivings, and Father Patrick Gahan reassured me by saying, "You are the only one here who has a book published". Thus, I bravely accepted the assignment and ended up enjoying it immensely.

Our names appear on the masthead as members of the writing group, but we aren't acknowledged individually. When I am asked if I wrote a particular piece, I take credit, being too vain to deny it. I don't think it's considered sinful to violate the rule if asked, but we do not ordinarily acknowledge it.

This experience had a healing effect on my self-confidence. I found out that I could produce what I was assigned and my experience in the craft helped me turn my work in with little editing needed. The very few who did know I wrote them gave me much appreciated compliments.

When I first moved to Wimberley, and I found myself in activities that challenged my mind, and my interest impelled me to jump in with my ideas and opinions, yet I found myself hesitating. I was out of practice and my short-term memory didn't function well, and sometimes I reached for a word and couldn't find it. This was surprising to me; words still came quickly when I was writing. They popped into my mind out of nowhere as if some unseen dictionary was cranking out what was needed before I even knew what I was seeking. This occasional glitch in my oral skills made me feel uncertain; add to that the self-doubts already present, and I could not enter freely into discussions although I was eager to do so. There was always present that self-doubt.

For my birthday each year, my daughter Sharon gives me a reading from her close friend psychic Anna Carter. Anna said that this year I would be speaking—delivering the message I was intended to bring. If I avoided doing this, I would be failing to complete the task I was to do in this lifetime. I wasn't surprised to hear this because I thought it meant finishing the book; it never occurred to me that it meant speaking orally. I was certain I would not be called upon to do that because at the time I doubted I could do it.

Anna even mentioned the time of year that this was likely to happen. To my surprise a number of things happened that did indeed involve my speaking about synchronicity, and they were clustered around the period of time she had mentioned. I found myself speaking about synchronicity at the Cursilla reunion one weekend. This occurred the same weekend my meditations came out on the Internet. I had also brought copies of previous printouts as hand-outs people might choose to read, and every one of the meditations were taken by group members. The copies ran out and some of the people who didn't get one requested I send them copies later.

On Tuesday of the following week the first of three workshop sessions on writing one's memoirs began at St. Stephen's. My good friend Mary Anne and I designed it for Art's Alive, a committee of people interested in various forms of the Arts. It had been organized at the minister's request to promote activity in any of these areas of interest. Mary Anne and I were members of this group as well as the Meditation Writers, and we co-presented a workshop entitled "I Remember When" that taught how to write one's life story.

I was a little afraid at first because I had not designed or presented a workshop in many years, and both Mary Anne and I were were far past retirement age. Could we deliver? I need not have worried; the workshop turned out to be very successful.

Anna was certainly right—I spoke and I knew that what I was doing served a purpose. Spirit was expressing through us.

***

The next challenge arose from another visit to California that happened after my "croning" ceremony. This year the trip was special because my granddaughter, India, had been through a crisis of major proportions and had come out on the other side. It also involved my speaking from my heart.

India is a beautiful and capable young woman and has been very successful in her career as a very sought-after hair stylist. However, last year we had been surprised and worried when she emailed us that she had decided she was an alcoholic. She admitted she had been drinking secretly for a long time and had finally faced that fact and had begun attending Alcoholics Anonymous. She had dived into the program and found a completely new way of life. Not only did she attend regularly, she changed her life and also got in touch with her Spiritual feelings. The partying and fast life she had been living had changed into one of service as she helped others who needed help along their way.

She told us how terrified she had been when she first stood before that crowd and admitted her alcoholism and what a relief it had been to do so and to be lovingly accepted by those who were there. She went on to say that she had been initially turned off by some of the people who attended the meetings, and how wonderful she found them to be when she discovered who they really were—their true selves. She now loves and admires many of the very ones she had first seen as people to be avoided.

We were able to see these people through her eyes when we attended a special meeting with her on a trip to California to celebrate the completion of her first year of sobriety. This meeting honored all members who were celebrating a birthday—an occasion when they had achieved a certain number of years of abstinence. We were to present India with the traditional cake representing one year of sobriety.

On the way to the meeting I was reminded that Sharon and I were both expected to give a little speech. I was undoubtedly told this prior to that time, but somehow it hadn't registered. I rode to the meeting trying to organize what I wanted to say. When the time came, I spoke of my own life—how I had seen how alcoholism could damage not only the alcoholic but also those who loved that person. I said that in my role as a counselor I had been so grateful to be able to refer my clients to A.A. when they needed to be terminated from my care, and I ended by saying that now I was able to rely on them as members of A.A. to help my own wonderful granddaughter.

I looked at the audience intensely at that point because I wanted each one of them to know how much I appreciated them individually and the organization as a whole, and I felt like what I had said hit home. I realized later that it was my therapist-self that had spoken because I wanted to help them see their own worth and importance as well as honoring India.

That night India gave a wonderful party, and Doc and Amanda played their guitars and sang their own original music. While we were visiting before the music started, a man came up to me. His said his name was Jeremy. He told me my talk had been very inspiring to him and he asked if I would give him a hug. Of course I hugged him and listened as he told his story.

He had been so addicted to different kinds of drugs that he had almost killed himself. Doctors had said they had nothing more they could do for him. Somehow at this point, he found Alcoholics Anonymous and those recovering addicts took him under their wings. They encouraged him, looked after him, and gave him the kind of loving support only they can give, and he was saved from the brink of death. When he finished talking and started to leave, he asked me if I would give him another hug and needless to say, I did. I was touched deeply by his life story, and one thing that meant a lot to me was the fact that my words had been inspiring to him.

When I was talking later to India about our conversation, she said, "Grandmommy, I'm the one who taught him how to hug! At first he was as stiff as a board and couldn't allow closeness, but now he loves to hug. He's doing well and we've all looked after him; once he missed a meeting for a good reason, but we checked on him to make sure he was okay."

I later said I felt like dedicating the book to him because he had demonstrated that my words could be inspiring; I finally decided to do just that. I mean it as a salute to Jeremy who turned his life around with help, but he can also serve as a symbol for all the people out there who need a hug—who need nonjudgmental acceptance, a helping hand and love.

I have written this book in hopes that my words will inspire other troubled and struggling people to discover the Spirit that created them and continues to create them can enable them to change from self-destructive ways and become more of who they were created to be. They can learn to utilize the strength and help that is theirs for the asking. In this way they can create a better life for themselves and help others also find their way.

The twelve-step program Alcoholics Anonymous presents is a succinct set of rules for creating a meaningful life. I know India's way has not been easy, but she has continued not only to work her own program but she now has "sponsorees" (addicts new to A. A). She is always there to help when need be). She also speaks at different clubs to inspire others to keep their sobriety. We are very proud of her.

THE GIFT

I found blue pebbles
scattered on the earth
and marveled at
their beauty.
I wondered what
they had to say to me.
In the dark stillness of night
I heard,
"Be kind to one another.
Do not be afraid.
Differences are only surface deep.
Look within and
you will find
at the core of your being,
you are all the same."

Your unique gift
is your Divine Purpose-
not meant for hording
but intended
to be shared.
Your precious gift
can help create
a consciousness of love.

Chapter 13
The Book Dream

I hadn't been writing for a while, having fallen into the mire of my doubts about exposing my belief system and violating my sense of privacy. Then I received a dream that jolted me into action.

Scene 1: The book appears to me as if presented in finished form. It was large—the size of a scrapbook—and the cover was red velvet. A gold line formed a border around the entire edge. Then I realize that it is covered with a layer of white dust. Suddenly a disembodied hand sweeps the dust off in one swoop.

Scene 2: Someone unseen asks me what the book is about, and my answer is misleading. I answer that is written about psychological material taken from workshops I had done as a therapist. A friend is standing to my right; she corrects me by saying, "I know about that book; that isn't what it's about. It is about your dreams."

Scene 3: *The book is being given to a group of women vaguely to my left. Above them and to the right is a rectangular wall hanging made of gray netting. On it is an image of a vase filled with flowers made of gold.*

I had awakened "knowing" that this was a message that I was to finish the book. I felt shaken and amazed at the clarity of it. My reply to the question about its contents had been evasive, revealing my resistance to the true message it was written to convey.

The woman who corrected my answer was a very intuitive friend with whom I have shared a lot of my kookiness. She has always been much more open than I in admitting her viewpoint on life. Incidentally, her nickname is "Wendy" from the character in Peter Pan, and she always hastens to explain that it is not "Windy". The explanation of her nickname is indicative of how often others misunderstand and distrust the utterances of intuitive people.

The symbolism of the size and flashy color of the dream-book reveals its importance to me. I don't usually remember the colors in my dreams. Dream labs have found that everyone dreams in color, but the dreamer commonly forgets the color. The red color of the cover speaks of the masculine principle described by Jung that is typically an aggressive attitude rather than a passive one and is also connected with "the word". Clearly, there was nothing sheepish about the appearance of that book!

At first I missed the significance of the movement from right to the left as it is given to the small group of women, but I have come to believe that it means it emerged from the right, intuitive brain which would mean it contains a lot of intuitive material. The book will be particularly helpful to anyone who is in need of recognizing the existence and value of the feminine principle. If the reader is a woman, it could serve to help her recognize the value of her feminine nature and unfold her "animus"–the potential for developing her masculine principle. If the reader is a man it could help him recognize and appreciate his "anima"–the artistic, feeling, nurturing, intuitive side of his own personality that he may not recognize or appreciate.

My reaction to the wall hanging was negative; it was an ugly gray and full of holes. There was no consistency to the shape or placement of the holes, and I missed the meaning for a minute. Then I realized that it had functioned like a fishing net; even the irregularity of the pattern spoke of the intuitive—which is never orderly and can't be trusted to always be correct. The gold in the vase and flowers had been seined out through the net. The symbol of the vase is feminine because it is a container; the gold appears to be thick and rather rounded indicating its value. This reminds me of Jung's intense interest in the ancient study of alchemy which involved attempting to change ordinary matter into gold. He saw this as a symbol of transformation. As far as my book was concerned, I knew that the gold represented the wisdom that had distilled out from my life experiences, and that is the true subject matter of the book.

Of course this dream inspired me to start writing again, yet I still struggled at times over whether to complete it. The major difficulty at this point was to arrange it into some sort of order. I was becoming increasingly aware of the underlying theme of spirituality and I still hadn't resolved my reluctance to discuss that. However, one day I happened onto the Biblical warning that if one denies

God, He will deny you. That really hit me. Some people may find it easy to speak of their Christianity; for me it wasn't. Perhaps it was because I knew how many people were turned off by organized religion and I certainly could relate to that.

I had also regained my spiritual belief through meditation and this was such an inner experience. I had come to know that my connection with God resided within my very being. Who wants to try to explain that?

The morning following that dream, I awoke engulfed in its impact. I decided once again that I was meant to finish the book—same verse—the hundredth time. I was so accustomed to my roller-coaster ride about completing it that I decided I must make a serious commitment. I also knew that rites have a way of being "heard" by the unconscious mind because they are symbolic; therefore I did something like a ceremony and pledged to complete the book.

After that I went about my daily routine. An hour or so later the phone rang. It was the Methodist minister from Brackettville, Rev. Jean Reardon. She had moved to Brackettville shortly before I had moved to Wimberley: I had met her as a fellow Rotarian and we have friends in common. Evidently one who was close to both of us had said something about what I was writing. The morning I received her call I was completely surprised—it even took me a moment to recognize her name. She said, "Frances, I'd like to ask you to come to Brackettville and speak to the Rotary Club about your new book."

I was flabbergasted; I couldn't imagine how she even knew about the book, and I knew it wasn't even finished. However, we had a mutual friend who must have told her about what I was writing. I explained to her that it wasn't finished, but she didn't give up. She suggested I talk about writing in general if I couldn't talk about the book; I replied that I'd think about it and call her back.

I brought myself back into focus by realizing that as a Rotarian she had to take her turn at providing the programs. When I had been a member of that Rotary Club, I had been in the same situation; I could sympathize. Yet my mind had to adjust to the shock of hearing her request. I have always been something of a ham and liked to give talks, but I also realized that I do it so infrequently now that I'm not as skilled as I once was. Would the words be there when I called on them? Old age can mean that the most ordinary of words can sometimes hide from awareness, and I can forget some point that is needed to tell my story (whatever it might be) effectively.

The part of me that wanted to do it said, "But this would be an ideal audience—you know them—you've spoken several times in the past to them. Give it a shot." Actually, I wanted to accept and more importantly, I felt I was not only meant to speak, but the subject should be the new book. The talk should not be about writing but about the unfinished book. This would solidify my commitment. I returned Jean's call and said yes.

The first step was one I had faced unsuccessfully many times before. How would I shape my confetti into some reasonable form? Somehow I knew I could do it, but I certainly didn't have it done even as the appointed day neared.

Two days before I was due to leave for Brackettville, the key to my car would not turn in the ignition. The final stage of an impending problem had manifested. It had happened before but had previously given way to mighty tugs on the steering wheel; this time the key refused to budge. I called my son to help, but he couldn't get it to move either. We called a man from the nearby town of San Marcos, and he had to replace the ignition entirely. With that accomplished we thought the car was in good shape for the trip; however the next day my car began moaning when I moved the steering wheel. This proved to be a major problem. That car was not to be driven in that condition and required an expensive and time-consuming repair. I had no car to drive to my intended destination.

Did this mean I wasn't supposed to go? Had I made the wrong decision? Despair descended upon me at this point. An inner argument began:

> The one who wants to go: "I don't want to call and cancel!"
>
> Objector: "They can always find a substitute. It's no big deal."
>
> Goer: "It is too a big deal! I'm supposed to do this!"
>
> Objector: "You're blowing this all out of proportion. Maybe you're wrong about being supposed to do it."
>
> Goer: "I'm going to call in Fair Witness." I do this and ask her, "What should I do?"
>
> Fair Witness: "What kind of alternatives are available?"
>
> Goer: "I could rent a car."
>
> Objector: "Rent a car! That's outrageously expensive and you have the repairs on your car to pay."

Goer: "I can do it."

Objector: "I can't believe it — that's ridiculous!"

Fair Witness: "Why do you feel it is so important to go?"

Goer: "I need to. It means I am really committed. If I tell that group about the book I really will have to finish it. I'll also get a first hand reaction to the content. If they are interested it will inspire me to finish."

Fair Witness: "You have your answer. If you had said you wanted to go merely to indulge the ham in you, the answer would have been no, but as an example of commitment, the answer is to rent a car and go."

Problem resolved. "Thank you Fair Witness."

I rented a rather small car and took off as scheduled the following morning. Before I left, I happened to notice a book entitled "The Tao of Psychology; Synchronicity and the Self" on my bookshelf. Dr. Jean Shenoda Bolen, the Japanese-American, Jungian psychiatrist, had written it years ago. I picked it up and thought I'd look over it when I got to Brackettville to see if I had forgotten something I should cover in my talk. I thought it was a copy given me by my friend Sheila Fling. In fact I could remember her saying, "This might be something you could use."

That small car had a pickup grossly speedier than my older, heavier model. It wanted to take off like a canon shot and it insisted on flying down that highway. It had no cruise control, and my driving consisted of fighting to stay at a reasonable rate of speed while driving west squinting to see the speedometer in the blinding sun. However, I arrived safe and ticketless shortly after lunch.

I was staying with my friend, Anna Renken, at Fort Clark, and she had already left for work the next morning when I took my notes and the Bolen book and settled at the table to force myself to come up with an outline for my talk. No one I have ever known would allow herself to arrive at this point apparently so unprepared, but I knew my subject well and all I needed was some key words. However, I had tried and tried to get this talk into an outline, but it refused to fall into an organized, step-by-step pattern.

I opened the book and on the first page was Bolen's very self-confident statement: "Don't expect this book to be linear–." No wonder I had struggled so much trying to organize my material; it was an impossible task! I felt great relief at recognizing that fact. I continued looking at her book and admiring her far superior knowledge and brilliance and worrying about my inferiority. I had to remind myself that I was just writing about my life and my experiences, and that couldn't be compared to her presentation.

In leafing through the book, I opened it to the front page. Words in Bolen's own hand jumped out at me: "Dear Frances—" For one crazy second I tried to make the name into that of my friend's instead of my own until I realized that this was the book that I had purchased years ago in Houston when she spoke at the Jung Center there, and Bolen autographed it! A synchronistic event!

When I recovered from my sense of shock, I was able to quickly dash off that illusive outline I needed for the talk.

This time it was no problem. Then, I dressed and left for the meeting.

Visiting in Brackettville and at the Fort is always like returning home although I have adjusted to my new home in Wimberley and am very happy there. This visit was special because for the first time I had returned early enough in the week to include the Rotary meeting. I had been a member and attended weekly meeting for years. Seeing old friends was great fun and meeting the new members was interesting.

Then, an amazing thing occurred before the meeting began. A member sat close enough for me to hear her discussion with her neighbor. To my amazement, she told a surprising story about her recent return from a trip to Europe. She had met a man on the plane who was on his way back to the States from Denmark, and she had just come in from Italy. They got into a discussion and found out that they were both from a tiny town in Texas where only five families lived! She had given me a perfect example of a synchronistic event, and I incorporated it into my presentation to help define the unfamiliar word "synchronicity" and illustrate it's meaning. If you think about this closely, you'll realize that my hearing it was also synchronistic event.

I had waited anxiously for the business part of the meeting to finish so that I could do my thing. As time moved on, I realized that I was not going to have nearly as much time as I had expected. To hell with the long-suffering outline—I would just have to wing it. The new member's synchronistic event served as a little jewel that caught the listeners' interest. Soon they were thoroughly caught up in my story.

The one issue in putting together my talk involved the theme of my spiritual journey, which I had come to realize was the essential thread that tied it all together. It could not be denied. My old hesitancy to speak of my spirituality still ran through my thought processes, but I did not let it deter me. One thing that bothered me was that a dear friend of mine who was in the audience was an atheist, and I knew he would be turned off by this revelation. In the past, that reluctant part of me would have avoided the subject. I could use the excuse that I was talking to a service club, not a church, and that to speak of my spirituality was inappropriate, however I knew I had to build my presentation around that rather than avoid it. I must admit I didn't sound as forceful as an evangelizing preacher, but I included it, and I was pleased with what I said. My atheist friend grimaced, but he didn't roll over and die.

As I spoke I realized people were listening intently to what I had to say, and that convinced me that they were really eager to know about their own inner life—particularly their dreams. They were also fascinated with the examples of synchronicity. The talk was a success.

***

A large part of the joy of visiting is always being with past neighbors and dear friends where I had lived. The custom in my particular neighborhood is to celebrate birthdays with a party and I was able to attend one the following evening. The occasion was joyful but particularly poignant since one of our most precious members had recently passed away after a long illness.

The next morning after the party when I was still enmeshed with the mood of the previous evening, I arose to write an inspired poem about this occasion and delayed my departure to give a copy to the friends who had given the party. Several others wandered in, and we had one final and unplanned get together before I left. The whole visit had proven to be particularly meaningful.

I finally boarded my flying steed and headed home. One last small mysterious thing happened on the way. I needed to bring the car back with approximately the same amount of gas as when I left—half a tank. I stopped a little way from my destination to buy gas. I had put my credit card in the slot and had begun fueling when I realized that the mechanism that ordinarily registered the amount of gas and the cost simply did not work. Then, I realized that this tank would be much smaller than the one in my car; I would have to guess at the amount in the tank. I immediately stopped fueling and hoped I was somewhere near the amount I should have. When I arrived at my designation and checked the gage, it registered exactly half a tank. Intuition had again served me well.

After I reached home I unpacked and returned the book to the shelf. Out of curiosity I looked for Sheila's book because I was so sure she had given me a copy, but I couldn't find it. Later, I mentioned the incident of the book to her, and she knew nothing about it. The only answer had to be that I had dreamt the whole scene of her giving it to me. I can only suppose that my dream-maker was trying to remind me of that resource. Intuition had called my attention to the non-linear aspect of the material that made it possible for me to finally outline what I wanted to say. I didn't use the outline for the talk, but it clarified my

thinking and gave me confidence in myself. I had received
another gift of Spirit.

If I had been writing fiction, the story could have not
been more artfully designed, and it would probably have
sounded too contrived to be realistic. Honor Spirit and
Spirit's gifts will exceed anything the human mind can
invent.

UNIT I. BIRTHDAY PARTY

We laugh and tease one another –
old friends gathered together in celebration
of one more year achieved
on this bumpy road of life.
Our gayety is tempered
by the loss of those whose journeys
have now ended,
leaving none of us unscarred.
We're shop-worn and weary,
some limp;
some must by-pass the cake,
yet we retain an inner vigor,
an appreciation of life.
We hold tightly
in weathered hands
the gift of our love for one another.
We know full well
how precious is each moment we share.
Come my friends!
Let's celebrate one more Birthday Party!

Chapter 14
Rebirth Time

I look at this stew that I have concocted and wonder what I left out and whether the pieces I have so carefully washed, pared, and cut to proper size can still be distinguished, or have I overcooked it all and made a big, gooey mess. And how does it taste—savory—too bland or too salty? What did I unintentionally leave out? I've slaved away over that proverbial hot stove cooking for a long time, and now I serve it to you. I can only hope you like your meal.

I have wanted to tell you that your inner spaces have a worth and meaning that is seldom appreciated but can enhance your life. To many people turning inward seems to be the wrong direction. Surely, they think, we should keep our focus on what lies ahead—on where we are going on our journey. That depends on the destination. Is it a place we want to reach? What if we arrive and find we've left a lot of our self behind? What if it's the wrong place altogether?

I suggest that what is important is to seek wholeness. Our strength and our potential lies within, waiting to unfold. It begins from the very center of our beingness.

By searching for and finding that center we discover inner resources we never realized existed. Most important of all, we find a source of wise guidance that is present and available because it is here that our connection to our Creator is located. Once that connection is found, we have only to ask for guidance and to be receptive to our good.

Dreams and meditation help us find that resource. We will never completely understand what we find in those dark, ephemeral spaces because we have finite minds, but we can discover what really matters in life and what is right for us, even when a glitzy, chaotic, fast moving outer world is supposed to be what is valuable.

Let's imagine that instead of a road that leads us ahead on our journey, admittedly with detours along the way, we travel in an upward movement as we encounter the things we need to learn in this lifetime. We may meet them again and again as we spiral upward in growing awareness, but each time we struggle with those challenges they become more refined. In this way we mature and unfold our own potential. We can learn from our mistakes.

It is essential to realize that as we encounter a time of choice we need to recognize the options and choose from wisdom rather than from an impulse to meet some desire or to choose blindly with no thought given to the outcome. The answer we seek can emerge from that inner wellspring of wisdom—that Higher Source rather than the ego.

The message intuited from the blue pebbles was of our inclusion in all that is—our connection with the whole of life, yet each of us is different. This in itself is amazing; think of it—there is, never has been, and never will be, another you. The same can be said of all of the other aspects of creation. How can we all survive unless we learn to tolerate, cooperate, and care for one another?

When human beings of different genders copulate and conception occurs, the fertilized cells divide again and again in the process of creating a child. The male was initially created to be larger and physically stronger than the female in order to care for her as she gives birth and nurtures growing children. Differences are ever-present and innate. Individually each human being has two hemispheres of the brain that operate in an opposing fashion; both are needed and have distinct roles to play in creative thought.

Two people can be in the same house; one looks out the front window, the other looks out the back. Each describes what they see and believes in his or her perception of reality. Unless they come together and realize there is a larger truth that encompasses both, they will be willing to fight to defend their particular position. Growth occurs when the tension between opposites becomes too extreme, breaks and moves into a new position incorporating some of each into the new creation.

A problem arises when compromise is regarded undesirable—weakness and shameful. It isn't a matter of giving in to the opposing side; it is a matter of the accommodation of differences. Compromise is honorable because it helps create a third place that can be agreed upon by both.

For me personally, this calls to mind the heading of a tribute to Eric after his death that appeared in the Brackettville newspaper and written by the superintendent of schools, Taylor Stephenson, who knew Eric as a fellow Rotarian. It read: "Eric McMaster was a Gentle Man". Eric was fully capable of being aggressive; his gentleness was not weakness. He served as a good example of a person who was respectful of others who did not agree with him, and he believed in compromise."

As I look back on my own life journey, I realize it hasn't been particularly easy to move from daddy's little princess to being a crone (and I do claim that status). I basically moved from a dependent stance (expecting others –mainly father figures—to provide my security) to discovering who I am one little step at a time. I assumed responsibility for my life. In doing this I became very familiar with that death/ rebirth theme. Ironically one has to first learn how to take on that responsibility then the next step is to realize the ego must give way to Higher Source in order to live fully.

I was making pretty steady progress until Eric's death. After that I was settling down to accepting a tranquil, rather lonely lifestyle that didn't match my Aries temperament. I came more alive when I was thrust into the atmosphere of Wimberley where I was a better fit.

When I first began sharing my thoughts and beliefs within the safety of my Jung study group, I was hesitant, almost afraid to speak. I had been too long in a place where I did not choose to talk about my mystical side. In the group I was able to let go of my façade and be me. In EFM we are called upon to share our life story. No one was horrified when I revealed the parts of myself I usually left hidden. All of this was very therapeutic. Slowly in Wimberley I became more in touch with my strength.

As I grew older, I had found my short-term memory was sliding into that black hole, and this contributed to my initial hesitancy to speak. Sometimes I reached for a word and it wasn't there, but I finally decided that many others had the same problem, and I quit worrying about it. It did affect my ability to remember my dreams, but I still tend to remember the important ones. One was particularly funny and it told me my animus still was alive and well.

Scene 1. I am on the second story of my own house. I decide to lie down and rest. It is the daytime, and I know that some people would frown on this, but I know that I have the right to do what I choose to do.

Scene 2. I hear my husband coming up the stairs. He has come home unexpectedly from work. I toy with the idea of having sex and invite him into my bedroom.

Scene 3: I see a toilet, and it is made of green porcelain. I look into it and see a shallow ledge within the bowl. Green peas are resting there having escaped the flushing.

I was amazed when I awoke and remembered that dream, then I started laughing at the absurdity yet the inherent accuracy of that symbolism. It had taken place on the second floor my house. The house would be my self, and the higher level would indicate where I was in my psyche. I had reached a higher level; I was an individual rather than a person defined by the expectations of others. I welcomed my animus—the part of me that could be assertive and could verbalize my beliefs and was capable of fighting my battles in an appropriate and effective manner.

Green is the color of growth, and those ridiculous green peas were round for wholeness and had provided a source of nourishment that had enabled my growth. They were

distilled out of the material I had taken in, and the dross
had been flushed down that commode. The peas reminded
me of the gold that had been seined out my life experiences
in the dream about the book. For one fleeting moment
I remembered my ongoing efforts at writing Pebbles and
thought: "I could change that title to 'Blue Pebbles and
Green Peas'." Needless to say, that was one choice I decided
not to make.

Speaking of such things as blue pebbles and green peas
shows how one must sometimes find the courage to tell
something embarrassingly personal in order to deliver one's
message. Like that dream-child who hung by her knees
from that balcony railing, one must sometimes risk ridicule
to tell one's story. Yet I have come to feel that my purpose
in life is to acknowledge and speak of the way Spirit
expresses in our lives when we open the door to our inner
resources.

It seems to me that the movement of Spirit is energy,
and I think people have become aware of that movement
in our modern society. Expressions such as "good or bad
vibes" have become part of our vernacular, and this refers
to feeling an energy flow and is intuition.

I believe the existence of that energy is God at work
in our life. It is present and easily recognized when we
experience caring for another person, feeling compassion
when they are hurting, or when we feel love for another
person. On a larger scale some of our finest moments as
human beings have occurred when an accident or a natural
disaster has happened, and society as a whole rushes to the
aid of victims.

In personal terms I have always felt that part of my
counseling ability arose from intuitively interacting with

my clients. I thought of it as "making a connection" with them. One drastic example of this became apparent to me when I worked in an observation room as a consulting therapist. In these situations the group or family who has asked for help knows they are being observed. They realize that it will be helpful to allow this to happen because it has been explained to them that the acting therapist can easily get caught up in the group dynamics and be unable to see what intervention is needed. An additional therapist sits in a viewing room and watches the session through a one-way glass window and calls in directives to the acting therapist through a microphone he alone can hear. The spectator's role is to point out patterns of interactions and possibly suggest how the acting therapist needs to move. As an observer I found this very frustrating, and when I examined my reactions I discovered that I had no "feel" for what was taking place. I also knew I could provide little help in that role.

One day when I was in practice, I opened the door to the waiting room and suddenly sensed negativity so pronounced that it felt like danger. I was to take in a new client and didn't know why the man had made the appointment, but it turned out that he was a court referral because he had been charged with raping the family baby sitter, a young girl. I vividly felt his hostility even though it was disguised, and I finally referred him to someone else because I felt I couldn't work with him.

I believe that one way we experience the energy of Spirit in a positive way is through creativity. When I suggest this, people often protest that they aren't creative. However, we think creatively when we do such things as put together a good meal, mend something, write a story for a homework assignment, plant a seed, or do arts and crafts. You are far more creative than you may have realized.

We use that energy negatively when we do such things as cause trouble, gossip or lie. These things can be harmful to others and to our selves.

Energy is involved when we open our self to new ideas, and when we move into a new way of being. These changes in our adaptation to life are not always smooth and certainly not always as amusing as those green peas. When we move forward in our unfoldment we may experience it as a death, yet rebirth follows inevitably. At that crucial moment of change, we may wonder if it is worthwhile for it can be painful. We may ask our self if we couldn't just stay the same—forget about seeking wholeness.

For instance when we decide to quit playing games and be up front with our partner, we will probably encounter resistance and perhaps anger. When you stop playing your side of it, the other person can't keep responding in the same old dysfunctional way. But we feel impelled to open that door, and once we have opened it, there is no turning back, and the beauty of our new life proves worth it.

I believe we live creatively when we are open to the energy of Spirit. This involves how we go about living and solving problems. Each member of my little family expresses this flow artistically. My grandson, Aaron, creates beautiful art work with wood, and works in a business that specializes in handmade, high quality rocking chairs of fine wood. My daughter is not only a massage therapist, she presents workshops on self-realization and is a professional artist. Her daughter, India, is a hair stylist and is now doing self-improvement presentations for fellow professionals as well as inspirational talks at A.A. meetings. I have painted and written all of my life. As I have recounted, Doc, my son, is a singer-song writer who has delayed recording his work.

When I first received the message that arrived via the blue pebbles, I had felt the urge to write about those revelatory dreams, but I hadn't begun the process. However things have now changed. My book is completed, and a few weeks ago Amanda, my granddaughter, finished producing a CD of her own music and lyrics started immediately after graduating from college. My son is now in the process of recording his voluminous stash of songs.

Every time we open the door to a new way of being we experience a rebirth. My son and I both heard the message that pebbles brought, listened, and acted upon it. I believe we are now literally in a new place where we will be actively sharing our gifts in a more expansive way.

***

Let me recount one last synchronistic event that occurred recently when I went with my friend, Sheila Fling, to A and M University for a weekend to hear one of the Fay Lectures series. Jungian psychiatrist Dr. Joseph Cambray spoke on synchronicity. His material came from a book he had written on the subject that was in the process of publication. A majority of the synchronistic events he reported were not personal experiences. They involved much larger incidences such as the discovery of penicillin and the Incan myth about the coming of a benevolent, bearded white man to the American continent that created an initial welcoming response to the Spanish explorer Pissaro.

On the way home Sheila and I were casually talking about where and when we had been at earlier times in our lives. During our discussion we discovered to our amazement that we had a mutual friend. We both had known Karinn Martin some thirty years previously. Karinn was not only my close friend; she was the therapist who had introduced me into the holistic therapy group mentioned previously. I had lost track of her after I retired and moved away from Houston.

On Wednesday of the following week, we both attended a meeting of a Jung study group. She arrived late and hastily sent me a note that said, "Synchronicity! Karinn Martin is at Deer Creek and is dying of cancer." She referred to a local nursing home where Karinn had been placed through Hospice.

Each of us quickly looked her up and joined a host of her friends from Austin where she had lived until she became ill three years previously and were helping to take care of her. Karinn had no family and we wanted to make her last days as comfortable as possible. She had remained alive unbelievably longer than expected, but the cancer had finally spread into her lungs. Sheila and I never doubted that we were sent by God to help her make her transition.

All of her friends lived in Austin, and the only nursing home capable of caring for her was in Wimberley. The helpers had to drive a long way to get there. One particular friend, Eudora Smith, had been assuming the formidable task of scheduling and staying with her almost every day, and she had to drive from the far side of Austin.

Karinn had been a vegetarian for years, and the regular nursing home fare upset her digestive system, so friends brought in special food. Each meal had to be retrieved from the refrigerator and served because the nursing home staff could not provide such individual service. By the end of her life we had to feed her. That angel of mercy, Eudora, had been spending endless hours tending to her. Someone closer at hand was sorely needed; Sheila helped in many ways but lived further away than I did, therefore I went there a lot in the evenings.

She wasted away into a pitiful little pile of bones with that horrible monster of distorted cells pinning her to the bed like a grotesque, triumphant wrestler holding down his prey. We watched her cling to her sanity, never complaining, never seeming to give up her hope for a miraculous cure— clinging to a life that must have been torturous.

Karin was born to a mother who lost her sight and hearing and a father who was deaf. Karinn's role from early in her life was to keep everything in their environment in perfect order so that they could cope. This created a compulsivity that possessed her during those last days. She knew where every item in every drawer in her room was located. As time went on, anyone who walked in the door of her room was asked to get something or move something. Just visiting with her was a challenge, and despite her unceasing gratitude for what we did, it created a difficult situation. It was challenging to step into a role of servitude so extreme; helpers had to constantly battle an impulse to rebel no matter how well they understood the cause.

Karinn was into positive thinking and she wanted to avoid discussing death. I knew of her need to reject any thoughts or words that she saw as negative, and I wanted to comply to her wishes while I was with her. After all—she had so little over which she had control, and control was so important to her.

Sheila, the daughter of a Baptist preacher, was comfortable talking to Karin about God and helping her face death, but I wasn't able to do this because I felt Karin put up barriers on this subject. However, as she neared death I realized there was something I did need to say to her. She had fought death so fiercely that I knew she must be terribly afraid, and I wanted at least to speak to her about death being a rebirth. Years ago we had spent hours discussing our spiritual beliefs. We had spoken about death as a transition in those days, and she hadn't been fearful then, but it's easy to speak about the end of your life as long as death is not knocking at your door.

What could I say that would get past her defenses and help diffuse that fear? I decided to speak of the unconditional love of God and about passing through that tunnel into the light. She knew about near-death experiences and that people who had experienced this often recount their reluctance to come back to this world after knowing such joy. I could remind her of that. I also needed to pass on the message that I had received from spirit again and again: "Do not be afraid".

I was literally writing the above paragraph and had stopped to eat lunch, and then lay down to rest when the telephone rang. It was a friend of Karinn's. The actual death process had officially begun; Karinn was dying. If I wanted to see her I should come soon.

I immediately drove to the nursing home with tears flowing. Even when we expect death, its eminence is always shocking. I encountered Eudora when I entered Karinn's room and we hugged each other, and I cried even while saying, "I'm so glad she's going." I then went to Karinn and leaned close over her to make sure she could hear me. I said exactly what I needed to say and then I said goodbye. I knew she heard me because she smiled.

I didn't return. Many other friends came to say farewell from then on until she died a couple of days later. The morning before she went, she announced to the nurse that this was the day she was going to die. She had finally come to terms with it. I was also told that at the very end Karinn looked upward as if seeing something and said, "Ready. Ready", and then departed this world.

I return home and when I began writing again I looked at the words where I had stopped and realized that Spirit had given me one more moment of synchronicity to relate. What a meaningful way to end this book.

I must hasten to add that I am old and know there's not a lot of time left on my journey, but that doesn't bother me. It does mean that I cherish every moment of every day as they whiz by. Crones don't fear death like other people, but when the time comes I may well quiver and run for cover. I hope I can remember then that it is my rebirth time, and I hope those who love me will really celebrate my passing.

REBIRTH TIME

I've seen a lot,
Have touched and tasted,
I've smelled the roses,
have eaten too much cake.
I've poked
in forbidden corners,
I've believed
unbelievable things.

Music has played
on my soul strings,
poetry has sprung
from my heart,
and I shall leave this place
grateful
for this lifetime,
and move joyously
into the Light.

All the mysteries
will be revealed,
and I will be
welcomed with love,
and best of all—
I will finally
get to look upon
the glorious face of God.

Made in the USA